THE ART OF THE DRUMMER

by

JOHN SAVAGE

Twelfth Edition

DEDICATED TO CAROL

Published by:-
John Savage's Music Books, 28, King George V ave., King's Lynn, Norfolk PE30 2QF.

CONTENTS

CONTENTS Continued

PREFACE

To the Student:

I have written in this book everything that I would teach to a student coming to private lessons with me. In the following lessons I have detailed the techniques that are the basis of modern drumming, I have taken these techniques and used them in a musical setting to form musical phrases and studies so as to inspire musicianship as well as technical ability. In developing these two factors (technique and musicianship) I believe that we open to the student the potential to express him or herself in musical terms on the drum set and this is the essence of all that I have to teach you here.

To the Established Drummer:

I have met many established, working drummers who have wished to enhance their knowledge of their instrument, and I hope that this book will bring forth the very best results. I believe that the most important factor in continued musical development is that each of us should always be ready to look again at anything concerned with the Percussive arts; So, be ready to learn again things that you may well be taking for granted.

You must be prepared to start again from the very beginning of the book and look at how well you are striking the drum—I have seen so many drummers who have never paid attention to this basic principle and found progression into advanced drumming impossible, you must be able to control your playing of the drum(s) in the correct manner in order to advance and also to obtain the best sounds from the drums.

If you have previously had difficulty in reading music then read each page of each lesson carefully, listen to the cassette of this book and look at the art of drumming in a new light—be methodical and don't get impatient if progress seems slow at first, persevere and you will achieve your goals.

INTRODUCTION

In this book we shall go through each step on the road to attaining complete control over the drum set and it is only by such control that you will be able to use the drums as a truly expressive musical instrument.

Some of the exercises and rhythms will come easily to you and you can put these into use in a group or band straight away, others may take days or even weeks to master properly, if it takes several weeks to play something at the right speed then the time given over to practice will have been more than worthwhile. If you can, set aside a certain time each day for practice, a regular half-hour or so will bring much better results than practicing for a long period once a week.

There are three points that you must remember at this stage : Firstly, read the notes on any exercise very carefully (if you have the cassette that comes with the book then listen to each exercise carefully). You cannot hope to master an exercise until you understand it and can picture in your mind exactly what you are trying to play.

Secondly, practice an exercise slowly at first until you can play it with confidence—Speed should come naturally with the mastering of each technique and cannot be achieved simply by getting faster and faster: *—note here that the correct approach to each exercise is to count-in slowly 1 2 3 4 and try to play the complete exercise at that speed without any mistakes or stops. When you can play the exercise through at least TWICE without mistakes then you can restart by counting in at a faster tempo and master the exercise at the new speed.

Thirdly, remember that all the exercises in this book are important so don't skip over those that you find difficult (or even those that look too easy to bother with)—the road to success is never easy so don't be discouraged if the going gets tough.

LESSON I

Reading music should be approached in the same way as reading a book or letter; you start in the top left hand corner and read from left to right. The essence of good sight reading is that you only play as fast as your eye can follow the written notation accurately. So reconcile yourself to the fact that a slow and methodical approach to playing will bring the best results in the long run.

All drum music begins with this sign ✏️ which is called the bass clef, this sign is also used for the bass line of a piano part and for low pitched instruments such as the bass guitar etc.

The bass clef sign is invariably followed by the TIME SIGNATURE (i.e. 4/4), for the present we will confine most of our studies to this 4/4 time (often called Common Time and written C instead of 4/4).

This time signature tells us that our music is counted 1 2 3 4 1 2 3 4 etc. Each group of Four beats is divided on paper by vertical BAR LINES, e.g.:

Count   1   2   3   4   1   2   3   4   1   2   3   4   1   2   3   4

Please note that the bar line does not signify any gap in music; it merely divides the notes up evenly.
THUS IN FOUR-FOUR TIME WE HAVE FOUR BEATS IN EACH BAR.

SINGLE BEATS (Crochets)

A single beat on the drum is called a Crochet and is written ♩
We can put four crochets into each bar of music like so:

Count   1   2   3   4   1   2   3   4   1   2   3   4   1   2   3   4

Now that we understand the Crochet we can play some exercises on the Snare Drum.
The Snare drum is Written in the middle of the five music lines (or clef).

Exercise 1

NOTE: double bar lines signify the end of an exercise.
To play Exercise One properly we must look carefully at the correct playing action for each hand. Firstly, we shall play exercise I(a) using the Right Hand drum stick only:

Exercise 1(a)

The tip of the drum stick should start approximately three inches above the drum head, the wrist is turned so that the stick strikes the head ONCE ONLY and then returns immediately to its starting position. You are using your wrist and fingers to control the stick as it bounces off the drum head (in a similar way to bouncing a ball). Make sure that you keep the beats equal in length and volume.

"(Crochets are also often called 1/4 notes. Thus four 1/4 notes constitute one bar in 4/4 Time)".

Exercise 1(b)

Now play the same exercise using the Left hand stick only.

The control required to play with the left hand is the same as the right. The Orthodox grip of the left hand is the most condusive to correct playing (see drawings), although if you find this too difficult you may hold the left hand stick the same as the right hand stick (called the Matched Grip).

The Action of the Left Hand Drumstick

Many Rock & Pop drummers use the **matched grip**. Each drumstick is held between the thumb and the index finger . Start by holding the drumsticks with the thumbs uppermost , then slowly rotate both hands inward slightly so that the back of each hand is visible to you and over the top of the stick . This way both hands can move naturally with the drumstick. Try to maintain a straight line from the elbow to the tip of each drumstick .

Exercise 1 (c) (Double Sticking)

Next we shall play this exercise using Double Stroke (two notes with each hand). First play Exercise 1c through RRLL, then play it again LLRR. It is important that you start many of the exercises in this book with either hand, this way you learn not to be dependant on one hand starting all the time, and you can also compare the sounds so that you can try and get each exercise equally good, regardless of which hand you are playing with.

```
R R L L     R R L L     R R L L     R R L L
L L R R     L L R R     L L R R     L L R R
```

Exercise 1 (d) (Single Sticking)

Finally, on the snare drum, we can repeat the exercise using Single Sticking, firstly RLRL and then LRLR. Try to maintain evenness of playing from both drumsticks.

```
        R L R L     R L R L     R L R L     R L R L
AND     L R L R     L R L R     L R L R     L R L R
```

NOTE that the basic snare drum exercise given to you here should be played at the beginning of each practice session. They are the fundamental basis of all good playing.

BUILDING THE FIRST DRUM RYTHM

We can now use Crochet notes to build-up a complete drum rhythm. Firstly, we play four crochet beats in each bar using the right hand drumstick on the RIDE CYMBAL* (Ex. 2).

Exercise 2

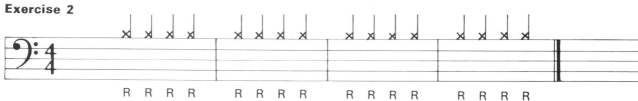

```
R  R  R  R     R  R  R  R     R  R  R  R     R  R  R  R
```

*Ideally, the ride cymbal you have should be 18in. to 22 in. in diameter and you should be able to hear the note of each drumstick beat above the ring or overtone of the cymbal. On many drum sets the ride cymbal fits on either a floor cymbal stand on the right hand side of the set, or on a cymbal arm on the right hand side of the bass drum as in the illustration. It is common to also add a second cymbal on a stand on the left hand side of the drum set which ideally could act as either alternative ride cymbal or a crash cymbal when needed (this type of cymbal is called a Crash-Ride and could be between 16in. and 20in. in diameter). Whereas, a Crash cymbal, is usually a thin cymbal, 16in. to 18in. in diameter which responds well when struck once with a fast Crash sound. If the drummer already has a Ride and Crash-Ride cymbals then his Crash will usually be placed to the Right of the Ride cymbal, often higher from the ground than the Ride

Exercise 2 (a)
To this ride cymbal beat we now add the left hand drum stick playing on the snare drum on beats two and four in each bar.

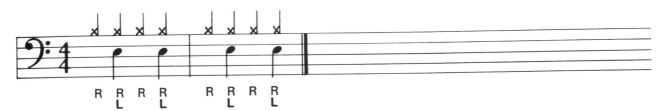

Your feet also play four beats in each bar, divided between the bass drum played with the right foot on beats one and three (written)

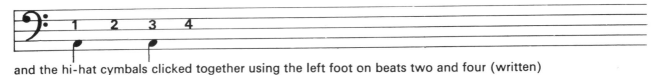

and the hi-hat cymbals clicked together using the left foot on beats two and four (written)

Put the two together to get Exercise 2(b)

Exercise 2(b)

When you can play exercise 2(b) evenly then start off with it s foot pattern and add to it the Ride Cymbal of Exercise 2(a), this gives us Exercise 2 (c).

Exercise 2(c)

Finally, we can add the snare drum on beats two and four to make our complete drum rhythm (Exercise 2(d)).

Exercise 2(d)

LESSON 2

QUAVERS

It is the understanding of quavers or half-beats that is often the first stumbling block for many drummers. A quaver, once played, lasts for only half as long as one Crochet (♩). Therefore, it follows that to make up one beat you would need to play two quick half beats (♫ = ♩). If you have difficulty in understanding this idea then imagine that you are learning a brass instrument like the trumpet for instance. You will blow for the full length of each crochet beat that is written but for a quaver you will only blow for half as long before moving on to the next note. If you can relate this idea of the note lasting on the drum in the same way as it would with a trumpet then you will be able to read any of the music that follows.

We begin our quaver studies with some snare drum exercises. For these exercises we write for snare drum only and there is no need to write in the five music lines.

Exercise 3

1   2   3 and 4

Exercise 3(a)

Firstly, we shall play exercise Three using *Single Sticking* (ex. 3a)

R   L   R   L   R   L   R   L   R   L

Secondly, we can play the same exercise using *Double stroke* for the two quavers.

Exercise 3(b)   **Exercise 3(c)**

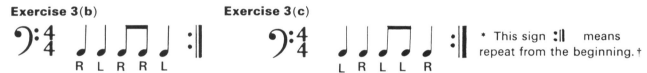

* This sign :‖ means repeat from the beginning. †

R   L   R   R   L   L   R   L   L   R

† If we do not wish to repeat from the beginning then we would put a reversed repeat sign in front of the place required, i.e.   ‖:   :‖

Exercise 4

1   2 and 3   4

Exercise 4(a) *Single Stroke*   R   L R L   R   L   R L R   L

Exercise 4(b) *Double Stroke*   R   L L R   L   and Exercise 4(c) L   R R L   R

Exercise 5

1 and 2   3 and 4

Exercise 5(a) *Single Stroke*   R L R   L R L

Exercise 5(b) *Double Stroke*   R R L   R R L   **and Exercise 5(c)**   L L R   L L R

Exercise 6

1 and 2 and 3   4

" Quavers are often called 1/8 th notes. Thus eight 1/8 notes constitute one bar in $\frac{4}{4}$ Time".

Exercise 6(a) *Single Stroke*   R L R L R   L   and **Exercise 6(b)** L R L R L   R

Exercise 6(c) *Double Stroke*   R R L L R   L   and **Exercise 6(d)** L L R R L   R

Exercise 7

     1   2   3 and 4 and

Exercise 7(a) *Single Stroke* R   L   R L R L   and **Exercise 7(b)** L   R   L R L R

Exercise 7(c) *Double Stroke* R   L   R R L L   and **Exercise 7(d)** L   R   L L R R

Exercise 8

     1   2 and 3 and 4

Exercise 8(a) *Single Stroke*   R   L R L R L   and **Exercise 8 (b)** L   R L R L R

Exercise 8(c) *Double Stroke*   R   L L R R L   and **Exercise 8(d)** L   R R L L R

Exercise 9

    1 and 2 and 3 and 4

Exercise 9 (a) *Single Stroke*   R L R L R L R   L R L R L R L

Exercise 9 (b) *Double Stroke* R R L L R R L   and **Exercise 9 (c)** L L R R L L R

Exercise 10

    1 2 3 4   1 and 2 and 3 and 4 and

Single Stroke

Exercise 10(a)   R   L   R   L   R L R L R L R L

and Exercise 10 (b)   L   R   L   R   L R L R L R L R

Double Stroke

Exercise 10 (c)   R   L   R   L   R R L L R R L L

and Exercise 10 (d)   L   R   L   R   L L R R L L R R

Although I have written some exercises with a repeat mark you may repeat as many times as it takes to gain complete control.

LESSON 3

BUILDING A POP RHYTHM USING QUAVERS

We can now build up several complete pop rhythms using a basic cymbal pattern of eight quavers to each bar; played either on the ride cymbal or on the top of the hi-hat cymbals with the right hand drumstick.
Firstly, play the eight cymbal quavers and on the first quaver of every four add the bass drum (right foot), so that the bass drum plays on beats one and three (ex. 11)

Exercise 11

When you are able to play this rhythm easily then you may add the left hand stick on the snare drum on beats 2 and 4 * (this means that for each group of four quavers on the cymbal the bass drum plays on the first half-note and the snare drum on the third).

Exercise 11(a)

* These beats are called the off-beats.

There are many variations of this basic pattern and we can now look at some of them.

You may note that the hi-hat clicked together on the 2 and 4 beats is optional ; you may find this easier so that you rock backwards and forwards on either foot; if this is the case then you should use this foot pattern throughout most of the exercises. If you want to play the ride cymbal part on the hi-hat cymbals then it is possible to obtain a distinctive swish sound by playing the left foot pattern as normal, or you may not want this sound and then you should keep the hi-hat cymbals closed but tap the heel of the left foot on the usual 2 and 4 to help maintain the swing.

In Exercise 12 we play two bass drum notes on the first two quavers of every four cymbal notes. Note that the snare drum sticks to its usual place on the third cymbal quaver of every four.

Exercise 12

In exercise 13 we vary the bass drum from a crochet to two quavers, so the bass drum plays 1   3 and

Exercise 13

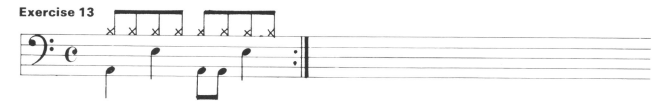

now we combine these two rhythms into Exercise 14.

Exercise 14

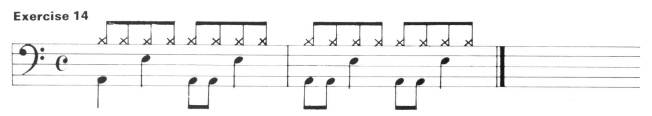

Exercise 15 is often more difficult to master at first, with the bass drum play 1 and 3.

Exercise 15

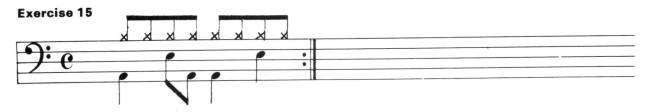

Once you have mastered Exercise 15 move onto Exercises 16 which has the same two bass drum quavers on both halves of the bar.

Exercise 16

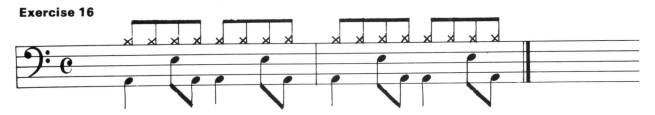

Exercises 17, 18 and 19 combine techniques learnt so far.

Exercise 17   (bass drum plays 1 and   and 3)

Exercise 18   (bass drum plays 1   and 3 and)

Exercise 19   (bass drum plays 1 and   and 3 and)

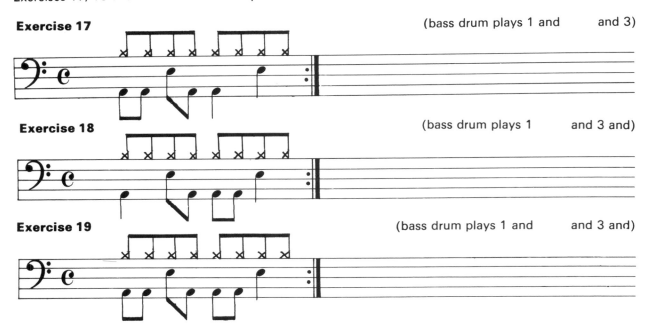

Position for playing basic pop rhythms

12

LESSON 4

EXERCISES AROUND THE DRUMS

We now have some exercises to introduce the small and large tom-toms.
The small tom-tom is written in the top space on the stave
The large tom-tom is written in the lower space
If possible keep your basic foot pattern going throughout these exercises (it is a good idea to set your feet in motion and count-in to the beat of the bass drum and hi-hat.)

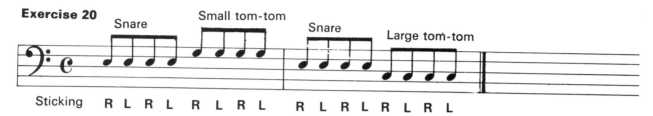

Exercise 20

This sticking is the easiest for this particular exercise, but once mastered try playing it through L R L R etc.
Then try R R L L etc. and finally L L R R etc.
Note that when you begin with the left hand stick it is sometimes necessary to cross one hand over the other to get around the drums ; I would reccommend that you follow the rule that the Right Hand will cross OVER the Left and the Left Hand will cross UNDER the Right.

Exercise 21

Sticking   R L R L   R L R L etc.
The same sticking applies to this exercise as to Exercise 20 so try to master all the possibilities.

Exercise 22

Use the same sticking for Exercise 22 as for 20 and 21

FILL-INS

Now we can put these exercises into rhythm patterns to make drum Fill-ins.
A Fill-in is any addition to the basic rhythm that is used to fill-out or enhance the music.

Exercise 23

Note that the easiest sticking is given, but also try L R ; R R L L ; and L L R R etc.

Exercise 24

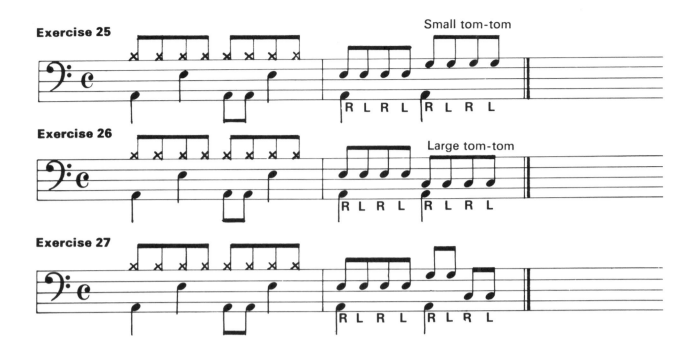

To conclude this chapter we shall play exercises designed to use the technical ability gained so far to play Musical Phrases, firstly on the Snare Drum and the finally on the whole drum set.

SNARE DRUM EXERCISES

The sticking for these exercises should be as previously given, i.e.:
Single Stroke: R L R L and L R L R *The Double Stroke:* R R L L etc. and L L R R etc.

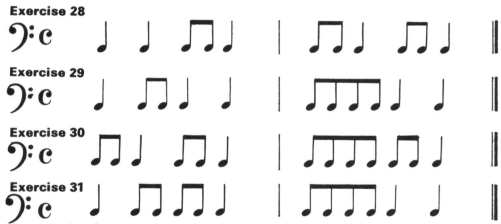

You may play these exercises in a variety of ways.
Firstly, play each exercise ONCE ONLY.
Secondly, play each through twice; this gives you four bar phrases.
Thirdly, play exercises 1 and 2 through without stopping in between (a) without repeats means a four bar phrase (b) with repeats means an eight bar phrase.

Fourth, play exercise 1, 2 and 3 without stopping; if you don't repeat each exercise then you are playing for six bars, if you play each twice then you have a twelve bar phrase.
Finally, playing all four exercises without stopping will give you (a) an eight bar phrase if you don't repeat and (b) a sixteen bar phrase if you do use the repeats.
The idea of playing these exercises is to develop your sense of musical phrasing, if you listen to most tunes they will show you how many musical ideas revolve around phrases that are four, eight, twelve, sixteen bars long and so on.

LESSON 5

SEMIQUAVERS

A semiquaver lasts for a quarter of a beat, which makes it only half as long in value as a quaver (half beat). One of the most common groups of semiquavers is to have four all together:

"Semi-quavers are also often called 1/16th notes. This is because sixteen 1/16th notes constitute one bar in **4** Time".

counted : 1 e & a

The 'and' on this comes in the same place as it would if you have two quavers

1 &

but the semiquaver group now has an extra quarter note either side of the second quaver. The four short notes would take up the same total time as either the two Quavers or one Crochet, i.e. :

 lasts as long as or

This formation is often followed by longer notes and we could easily add a crochet at the end and get :

1 e & a 2

This grouping is often called the FIVE STROKE ROLL* to play the exercise I would recommend that you beat in with the right foot, a steady 1 2 3 4 and keep this bass drum beat going as you try to master the five stroke roll. Note that the bass drum would come in on the first and fifth notes of the drum roll, so on these notes your foot and hand should be absolutely together.

Exercise 32

There are two usual ways of sticking this :

Exercise 32(a)   *Single Stroke*

R L R L R   L R L R L

*It is very important that the roll should start and end cleanly and positively.

Exercise (b)   *Double Stroke.*

R R L L R   L L R R L

*Note that the word ROLL at this stage does not mean that you should try to achieve some sort of fast, sustained buzz type of roll in the traditional sense of the word. This will be achieved later, but, for the present concentrate on crisp, clear, controlled notes at a slow tempo and leave "closing the Roll up" until later. Remember that speed comes only with complete control.

Exercise 33

We can replace the crochet in the previous exercise with two quavers and we arrive at the SIX STROKE ROLL.

1 e & a 2 &   3 e & a 4 &

Exercise 33(a) and Exercise 33(b)   *Single Sticking*

R L R L R L R L R L R L   L R L R L R L R L R L R

15

Exercise 33(c) and Exercise 33(d)   *Double Sticking*

R R L L   R L   R R L L   R L   L L R R   L R   L L R R   L R

Note that in this and other Even numbered rolls we lead with the same hand all the time, whereas odd numbered rolls, like 5, 7 etc., change from one hand to another.
Now we can try some snare drum exercises using semiquavers. Master each using single sticking first and then Double stroke.

Exercise 34

Single Stroke   R L   R L R L R   L R L R L   R L R L R   *when you repeat the left leads.

Exercise 34(a)   *Double Stroke*

R   L   R R L L R   L L R R L   R R L L R
L   R   L L R R L   R R L L R   L L R R L

Exercise 35 and Exercise 35(a)   *Single Stroke*

R L R   L R L R L   :| L R L   R L R L R   :|

Exercise 35(b) and Exercise 35(c)   *Double Stroke*

R L R   L L R R L   :| L R L   R R L L R   :|

*With all of the exercises it is important to keep the bass drum and hi-hat rhythm going underneath each exercise (this applies right through the book unless otherwise stated).

Exercise 36   Single Stroke

R L R L R L R L R   L R L R L R L R L

Exercise 36(a)   *Double Stroke.*

R L   R L R R L L R   L R   L R L L R R L

Exercise 37 and Exercise 37(a)   Single Stroke

R   L R L R L R L   :| L   R L R L R L R   :|

Exercise 37(b) and Exercise 37(c)   *Double Stroke*

R   L L R R L R L   :| L   R R L L R L R   :|

Exercise 38   Single Stroke

L R L R L R L R L   R   L R L R L R L R

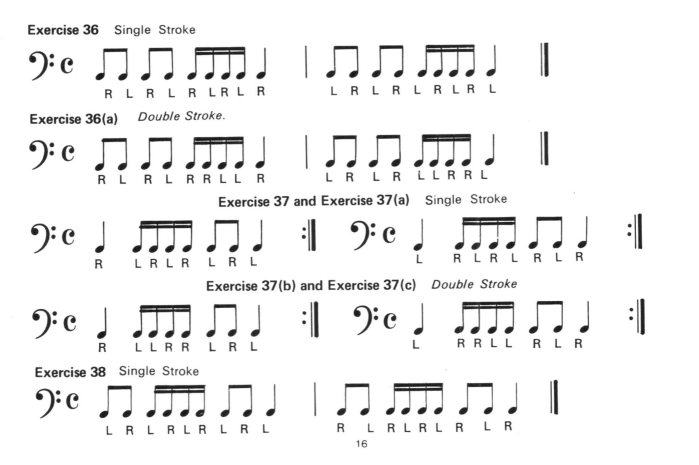

Exercise 38(a)   *Double Stroke*

Exercise 39 and Exercise 39(a)   Single Stroke

Exercise 39(b) and Exercise 39(c)   *Double Stroke*

We now play some two bar phrases using the material that we have learnt so far.. Although there are some four bar exercises later in this lesson, these earlier exercises give a four bar phrase when played through using the repeat sign.

Exercise 40   Single Stroke

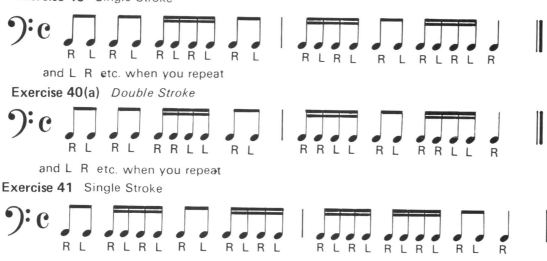

and L R etc. when you repeat

Exercise 40(a)   *Double Stroke*

and L R etc. when you repeat

Exercise 41   Single Stroke

and L R etc. when you repeat

Exercise 41(a)   *Double Stroke*

and L R etc. when you repeat

Exercise 42   Single Stroke

and L R etc. when you repeat

Exercise 42(a)   *Double Stroke*

and L L etc. when you repeat

Exercise 43 Single Stroke

Exercise 43(a) *Double Stroke*

Exercise 44 Single Stroke

and L R etc. when you repeat

Exercise 44(a) *Double Stroke*

and L R etc. when you repeat

Exercise 45 Single Stroke

and L R etc. when you repeat

Exercise 45(a) *Double Stroke*

and L R etc. when you repeat

FOUR BAR PHRASES

We now have four Studies that each give you a separate four bar phrase when played through once. If you want to repeat any of these then of course you will get an eight bar-phrase, if you want to play straight from one through the next then you will increase the length of the study accordingly. You will have observed that I use the term Exercise to describe a short piece of music designed at acquiring a certain technique and the term Study when playing a musical statement that gives rise to a sense of musical completeness in its own right. The sticking for these studies should be as before, one through R L, and L R, then R R L L and finally L L R R.

Exercise 46

Exercise 47

Exercise 48

Exercise 49

Phrasing Studies for the Drum Set

Exercise 50

Exercise 51

Exercise 52

Exercise 53

Exercise 54

19

LESSON 6

We can now play groups of semiquavers around the standard drum set. In exercises 55 to 60 we play various studies around the drums ; sticking is easiest with R L R L, but you should also try L R L R, R R L L and L L R R to help build up even greater technical skill.

The sign ⟋ means play the previous bar again.

These patterns are then put together to make two four bar studies, Exercises 61 and 62.

SEMIQUAVER STUDIES AROUND THE DRUMS

Fill-ins using semiquavers

We now move on to use semiquavers to create typical Rock Fill-ins amidst some of the rhythms that we have learnt so far. By far the easiest sticking for the fill-in is R L R L

Exercise 63

Exercise 64

Exercise 65

Exercise 66

Syncopated exercise

(not on cassette)

LESSON 7

VARIATIONS ON SEMIQUAVERS

Semiquavers do not always appear in groups of four. There are three very common variations that we shall try now. Firstly, we meet two semiquavers followed by a quaver ♫♩ remember that the value of each

lasts AFTER the note has been played therefore we have three notes in quick succession, the third note being a half beat, lasts for longer than the other two so it isn't until that half beat is up that we could play anything else. This phrase is counted   1 e &

You are, in fact, playing three notes the same as the first three of four semiquavers, but the last note sustains through what would normally be the fourth semiquaver like so :-

The easiest sticking for pop material is single sticking, but sometimes, when reading passages at a fast speed it is easier to play the two semiquavers both with one hand.

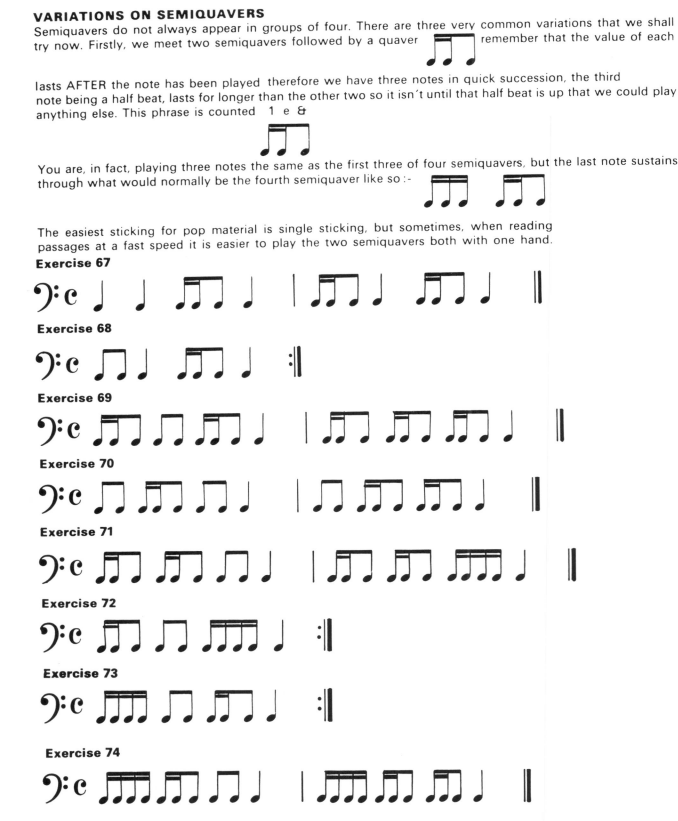

Exercise 67

Exercise 68

Exercise 69

Exercise 70

Exercise 71

Exercise 72

Exercise 73

Exercise 74

Fill-ins

Exercise 75

Exercise 76

Exercise 77

Secondly, we encounter a quaver followed by two semiquavers   1 & a
It is easiest to think of this group as being related to four semiquavers you play the first note, not the second, but play the third and fourth so you are playing the ONE AND A.

Snare drum exercises

Exercise 78

R   L   R LL R   L   R   L RR L   Easiest sticking

also
R L RLR L
and
L R LRL R

Exercise 79

R   L RR L   R   L   R LL R   L

also
R LRL R
and
L RLR L R

Exercise 80

R LL R   L RR L

also
R LRL   R LRL
and
L RLR   L RLR

Exercise 81

R LL R L RLL R L

also
R LRL R L RLRL
and
L RLRL R RLRL R

and L RR L R L RR L R

Exercise 82   Double stroke

R LL R L RRLL R | L RR L R LLRR L

Exercise 82(a) and Exercise 82(b)   Single stroke

R LR L R LRLR L :|| L RL R L RLRL R :|

Exercise 83   Double stroke

R L R L R LL R | L R L R L RR L

Exercise 83 (a) and Exercise 83 (b)   Single stroke

R L R L R LR L :|| L R L R L RL R :|

Exercise 84   Double stroke

R LL RRLL R L R | L RR LLRR L R L

Exercise 84 (a) and Exercise 84 (b)   Single stroke

R LR LRLR L R L :|| L RL RLRL R L R :|

Exercise 85   Double stroke

R LL R LL R L R | L RR L RR LLRR L

Exercise 85 (a)   Single stroke

R LR L RL R L R | L RL R LR LRLR L :||

Fill-ins using ♫

Exercise 86

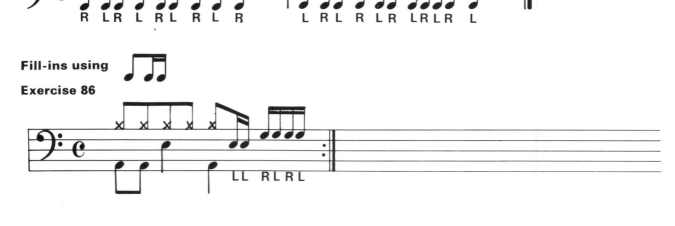

LL RLRL

24

Exercise 87

L L RRLL

Exercise 88

LL RLRL RLRL

The third variation on the semiquaver pattern involves a dotted quaver followed by a semiquaver
The dot after the quaver increases its value by half again
Thus a half beat becomes three-quarters of a beat in length, and is therefore equal to three semiquavers.

We often add a semiquaver onto the end of this three-quarter note to make up an even beat, the easiest way of thinking of this is as illustrated, compared to four semiquavers you would play on the First and Fourth notes.

In playing the following snare drum exercises the dotted quaver comes ON the beat and the quarter note joined to it comes just before the next beat.

Exercise 89

1   2   3 a 4

*Single sticking throughout.
If you keep the bass and hi-hat going
this should help you to count.

Exercise 90

1   2 a 3   4

Exercise 91

1   2 a 3 & 4

Exercise 92

1 & 2 a 3 & 4

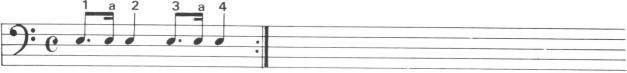

Exercise 93

1 a 2   3 a 4

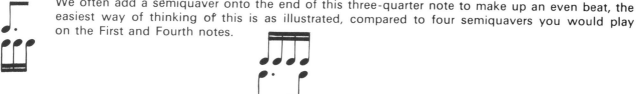

Exercise 94

Exercise 95

Exercise 96

Exercise 97

NOW WE WILL BUILD UP A STRAIGHT ROCK RHYTHM USING

Exercise 98

Exercise 98(a)

Exercise 98 (b)

Be careful to ensure that the second note on the snare drum falls in between the fourth and fifth cymbal notes but should not interfere with the flow of the cymbal rhythm.
Once this rhythm is mastered, we can play some variations on the same theme.

Exercise 99

Exercise 100

Exercise 101

Exercise 101(a)

Exercise 102

FINALLY SOME FILL-INS USING

Exercise 103

Exercise 104

Exercise 105

Exercise 106

LESSON 8

SWING ROCK

So far we have concentrated on 'Straight' pop rhythms based on an even eight quavers on the cymbal to each bar. We can now move on to study pop rhythms that are based on a dotted quaver—semiquaver cymbal pattern.

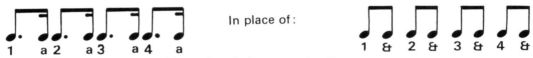

Note: the position of the cymbal beats in relation to each other.

Exercise 114

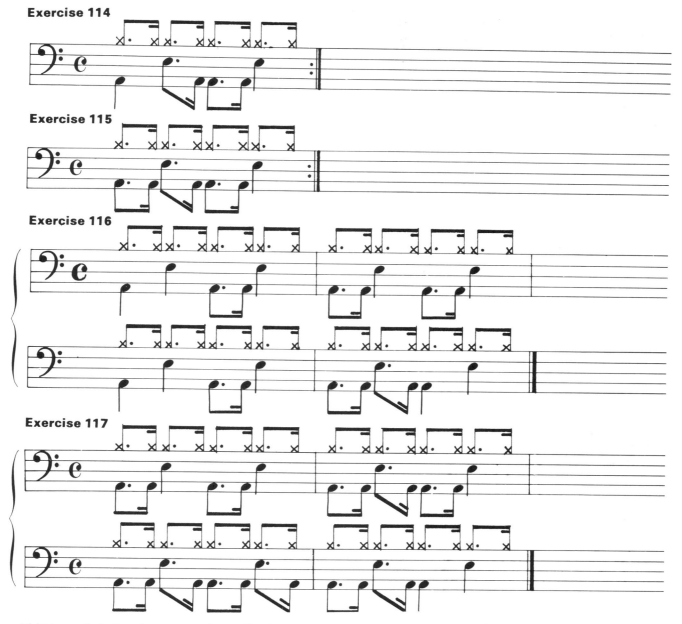

Exercise 115

Exercise 116

Exercise 117

This type of rhythm has two main applications, at a medium/slow tempo it is used for fox trot and country and western type tunes ; at a faster speed it is used for Rock & Roll.

If we vary this snare drum pattern to  we can play the rhythm slowly for Country and faster for Rock. For country and western we should probably rest the left hand on the snare drum head and play the stick across the rim : the right hand would play on the hi-hat and a nice clean sound is obtained with the tip of the drumstick, whilst the left foot holds the hi-hat cymbals tightly closed together.

Exercise 118

For Rock & Roll the left hand stick would play the snare drum in the usual manner and the hi-hat cymbal could be opened slightly to give a 'Thicker' sound, especially if you play the cymbal with the shoulder of the stick and not the tip.

LESSON 9

STRAIGHT HARD ROCK RHYTHMS

For these rhythms we will maintain a steady 1 2 3 4 played by the right hand stick on the hi-hat cymbal. Be careful not to let the right hand follow any of the patterns played by the bass drum. To perfect these rhythms it may be necessary to practice them at VERY SLOW speeds. This is not a bad thing. Practice as slowly as is necessary to play each rhythm CORRECTLY and then go on to play each at normal tempos once you have completely mastered each technique.

Exercise 119

Exercise 120

Exercise 121

Exercise 122

Exercise 123

Exercise 124

Exercise 125

SWINGY HARD ROCK RHYTHMS

We can now adapt the same cymbal four crochets cymbal rhythm, but this time we play the bass drum in a 'Swingy' style.

In these exercises I have combined the individual techniques to form studies, but you may study each bar as a separate exercise if necessary, and work towards playing each exercise as a whole.

Exercise 126

Exercise 127

Exercise 128

We conclude this section with an 12 bar study using some more intricate bass drum patterns that lend themselves easily to the semi-quaver cymbal pattern.

If you wish you may learn individual bars of the study and build up to playing the complete study.

Study

LESSON 10

TRIPLETS

The triplet sign (3) may be written over several different types of notes, but we shall commence our studies with triplet quavers ; counted 1 an er. Whereas a normal quaver lasts for half a beat, the triplet quavers last for a third of a beat each, with the three adding up to a total of one Crochet beat. You will often see triplets explained as three notes in the time of two, you will understand that three triplet or third notes add up to the total of one beat the same as two normal quaver or half notes.

$$\text{1 beat} \quad = \quad \text{2 halves} \quad = \quad \text{3 thirds}$$

Now we can play some snare drum exercises to develop our triplet technique, but you must bear in mind the sticking will vary much more from one hand to the other because we are now playing groups of three notes instead of twos or fours as previously.

Exercise 129

Exercise 130

Exercise 131

Exercise 132

Exercise 133

Exercise 134

Exercise 135

and Exercise 129 (a)

and Exercise 130 (a)

and Exercise 131 (a)

and Exercise 132 (a)

and Exercise 133 (a)

and Exercise 134 (a)

and Exercise 135 (a)

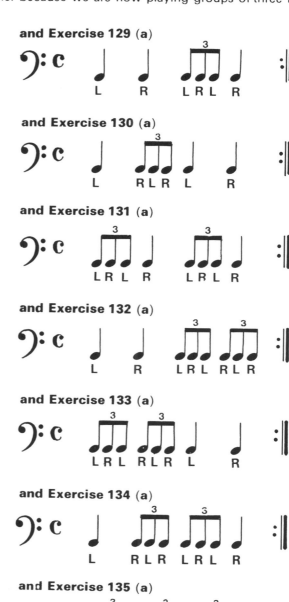

TRIPLETS AROUND THE DRUMS

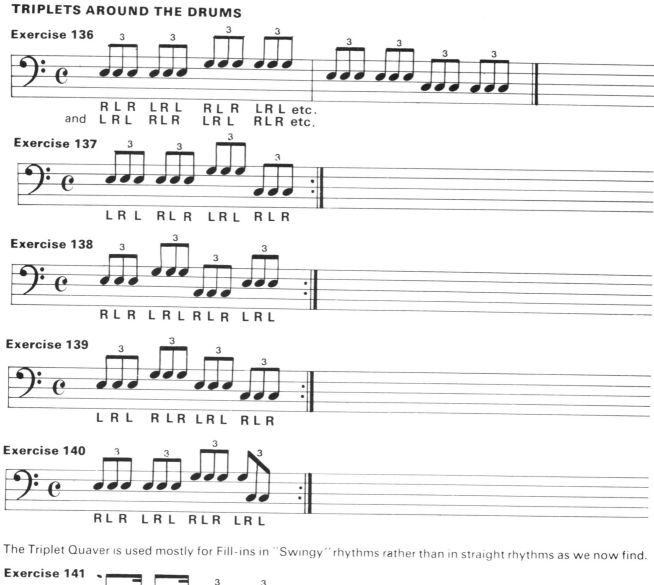

Exercise 136

R L R L R L   R L R   L R L etc.
and L R L   R L R   L R L   R L R etc.

Exercise 137

L R L   R L R   L R L   R L R

Exercise 138

R L R L R L R L R L R L

Exercise 139

L R L   R L R L R L   R L R

Exercise 140

R L R   L R L   R L R   L R L

The Triplet Quaver is used mostly for Fill-ins in "Swingy" rhythms rather than in straight rhythms as we now find.

Exercise 141

Exercise 142

Exercise 143

Exercise 144

LESSON II

JAZZ RHYTHMS

The swing type cymbal rhythm that we are now going to look at is used widely for jazz, quicksteps and fox-trots at slower tempos, etc. This cymbal rhythm is :

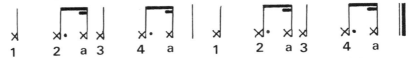

The basic rhythm is constructed much as before with the bass drum on beats 1 and 3, and the snare drum and hi-hat on beats 2 and 4 in each bar.

Exercise 145   **Exercise 145 (a)**
Play over until you are ready to play
the complete rhythm.

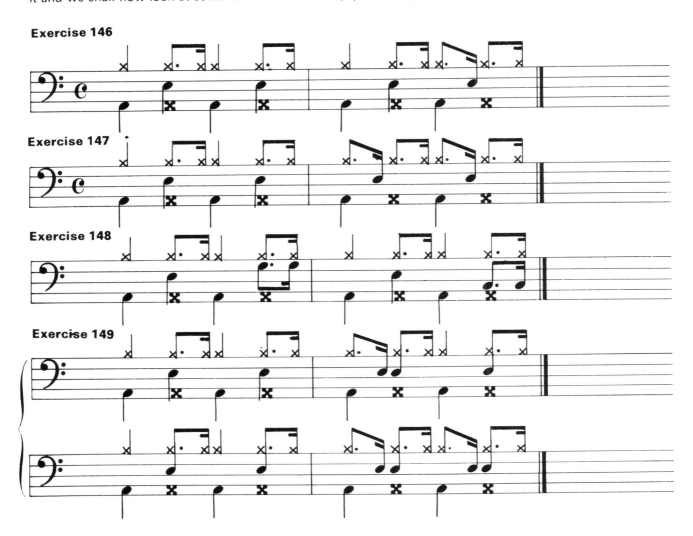

Be careful to *PLAY* all the Ride cymbal notes and not let the stick's natural bounce do the work for you. Note that the chick of the hi-hat cymbals on beats two and four is more important in this rhythm where the use of the hi-hat gives the rhythm lift. The Left Hand can change the feel of the rhythm considerably. If you play a strong 2 and 4 on the snare drum, as in Exercise 145 the rhythm fits very well with Traditional Jazz type tunes, whereas for more modern scngs the left hand snare drum pattern varies whilst the other limbs remain constant. The technique of controlling the limbs whilst the snare dum varies is one aspect of INDEPENDENCE as we know it and we shall now look at some exercises to develop your ability with this technique.

Exercise 146

Exercise 147

Exercise 148

Exercise 149

Exercise 150

Exercise 151

FILL-INS IN SWING RHYTHM
Exercise 152

Exercise 153

Exercise 154

Exercise 155

THE BOUNCE TRIPLET

Triplets fit with jazz rhythms just the same as with the Swing-rock that we studied earlier, but Single Stroke triplets are often too 'heavy' in sound and style for many songs, so we often use a sticking variation called the bounce triplet. The triplet is counted as before, but the sticking we will use gives the technique a much lighter sound.

Firstly, practice the bounce triplet on the snare drum.

Exercise 156

RLL RLL RLL RLL   RLL RLL RLL RLL

Be very careful to practice this technique slowly and ensure that ALL THREE BEATS ARE EVEN, it is very easy to find yourself playing the two left handed notes too close together.
Now we apply this technique around the drums, note how much easier it is to play odd tom-tom notes using this sticking.

Exercise 157

RLL RLL | RLL RLL | RLL RLL | RLL RLL

Exercise 158

RLL RLL RLL RLL

You might note that this technique is best played with the left hand stick playing close to the drum rim. Here the response is greatest and you can control the volume and sound of the Triplet

Exercise 159

RLL RLL RLL RLL etc.

Exercise 160

RLL RLL etc.

We can now use the bounce triplet for fill-ins.

Exercise 161

Exercise 162

The bounce triplet can also be used as an independent technique with the right hand remaining on the ride cymbal. In the following studies we begin with independence technique and move on to using the bounce triplet for both independence and fill-in.

Exercise 163

Exercise 164

Exercise 165

In order to write the next set of exercises correctly we must re-write the cymbal rhythm into triplet formation so as to show clearly how the cymbal notes come together with the snare drum beats in certain places. In fact, we have been playing this rhythm right from the beginning of the lesson, but the first cymbal pattern is the usual one that is written almost all the time; if the rhythm is to SWING or lift then you automatically play the rhythm in the triplet style, otherwise it would be too jerky to sound good, but as you will see it written mostly as a dotted quaver-semiquaver I have felt this the best one to begin with.

Exercise 166

*I must explain to you here that the sign ⅞ means that the middle note of the triplet is not played. This sign is explained fully in the section entitled REST NOTES that follows later in the book.
These points are really academic details that I don't wish to elaborate on, but feel they must be explained in order to make clear the exercises here.

Exercise 167

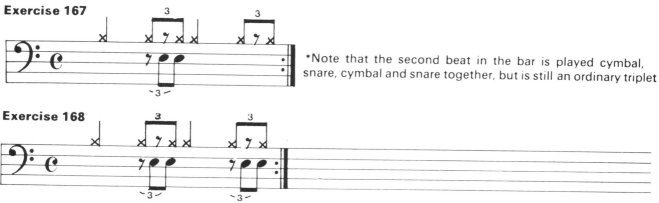

*Note that the second beat in the bar is played cymbal, snare, cymbal and snare together, but is still an ordinary triplet

Exercise 168

Throughout keep to the basic foot pattern of bass, hi-hat, bass, hi-hat etc.

Exercise 169

Exercise 170

Exercise 171

If you have difficulty with these exercises then start with this approach :—

Exercise 172

When you have this mastered add an extra cymbal note on the sixth note of each group of six ;—

Exercise 173

TWO STUDIES

Exercise 174

Exercise 175

LESSON 12

TRIPLET SEMIQUAVERS:

We can group together three semiquavers as a triplet and this adds up to a total of a half beat (two semiquavers). In the exercises written for you we play snare drum exercises first and then put these around the drums to form fill-ins in slow and medium rock rhythms. You should note that in exercises 176 to 181 the triplet starts on the half beat and this formation of notes should suggest that the group is leading into the fourth note which is on the beat, this leads to the beat being somewhat emphasised. However, when we reach exercise 182 the triplet starts ON THE BEAT itself and therefore any emphasis should be put at the beginning of the group.

Exercise 176

Exercise 177

Exercise 178   **Exercise 178 (a)**

Exercise 179

Exercise 180   **Exercise 180(a)**

Exercise 181

Exercise 182

Exercise 183

39

Exercise 184

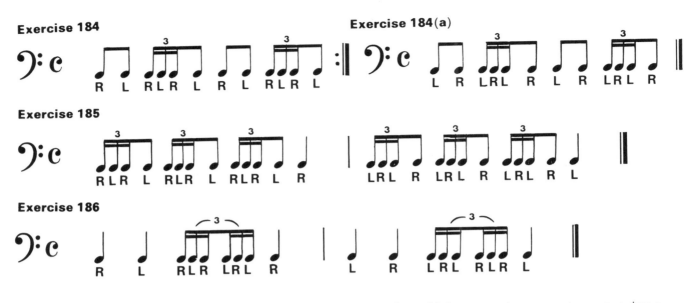

Exercise 184(a)

Exercise 185

Exercise 186

Note that on Exercise 186 there are two groups of triplets together which means six even notes occupying a total of one beat.

Exercise 187

Exercise 188

Exercise 189

Exercise 190

Exercise 191

Exercise 192

Now we move on to use these techniques for Fill-ins in slow and medium rock tempos.

Exercise 193

Exercise 194

Exercise 195

Exercise 196

In slow rhythms such as these we often vary the cymbal pattern to add interest. This type of cymbal rhythm is best played on a tightly closed hi-hat.

Exercise 197   **Exercise 198**

Exercise 199   **Exercise 200**

Exercise 201   **Exercise 202**

THESE RHYTHMS LEAD US INTO SOME MODERN 'FUNKY' EXAMPLES

Exercise 203

Exercise 204

Exercise 205

Exercise 206

STUDY.

LESSON 13

ACCENTS

An accent is usually written as a > written over any note that is to be played louder than the others. To accent single notes on the snare drum the stick should be raised much higher than normal by rotating the wrist further than for a non-accented note; this should be done wherever possible, whilst the other hand is executing the previous note so that the rhythm to be played comes out as evenly as possible. In order to bring-out the accented notes fully it is advisable to keep the volume of the other notes down so that they remain in the background whilst the accents particularly stand-out.   *(See Diagram).

Accenting with the right hand

Accenting with the left hand.

Snare Drum Exercises.

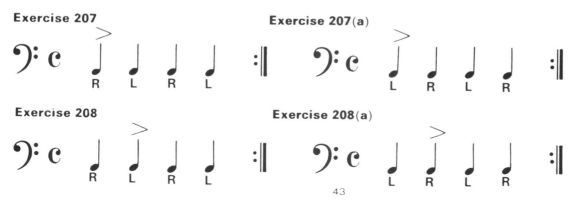

Exercise 207

R L R L

Exercise 207(a)

L R L R

Exercise 208

R L R L

Exercise 208(a)

L R L R

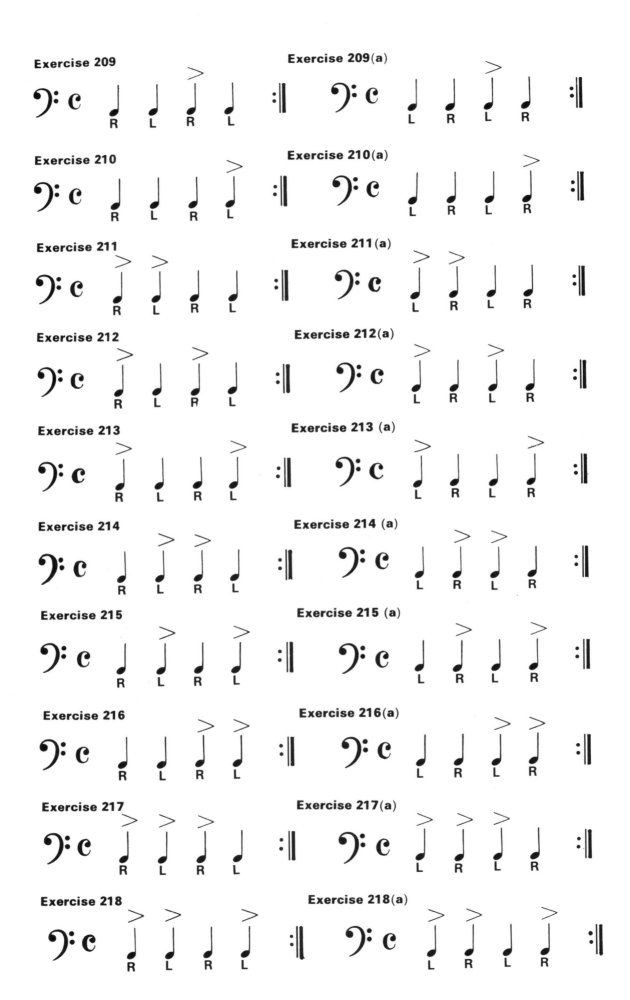

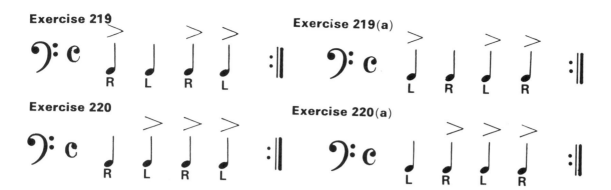

In the accent exercises that now follow I have written the exercises to start with the Right Hand, but you should also try each exercise starting with the Left Hand.

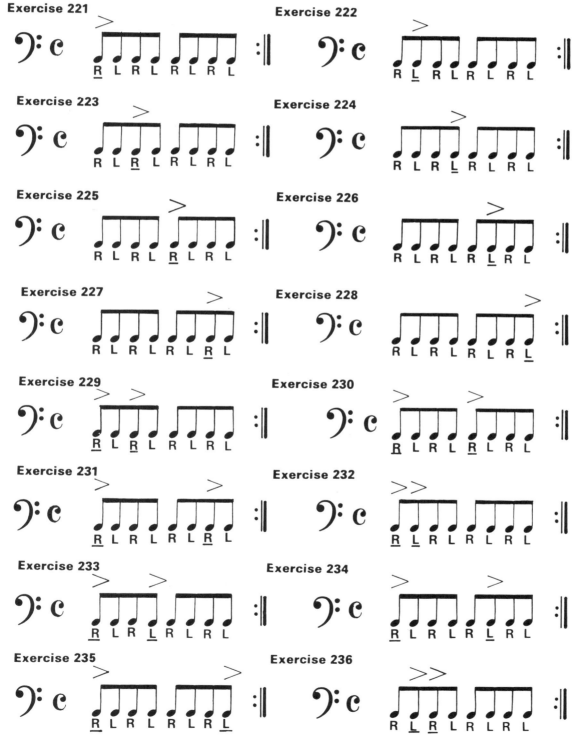

45

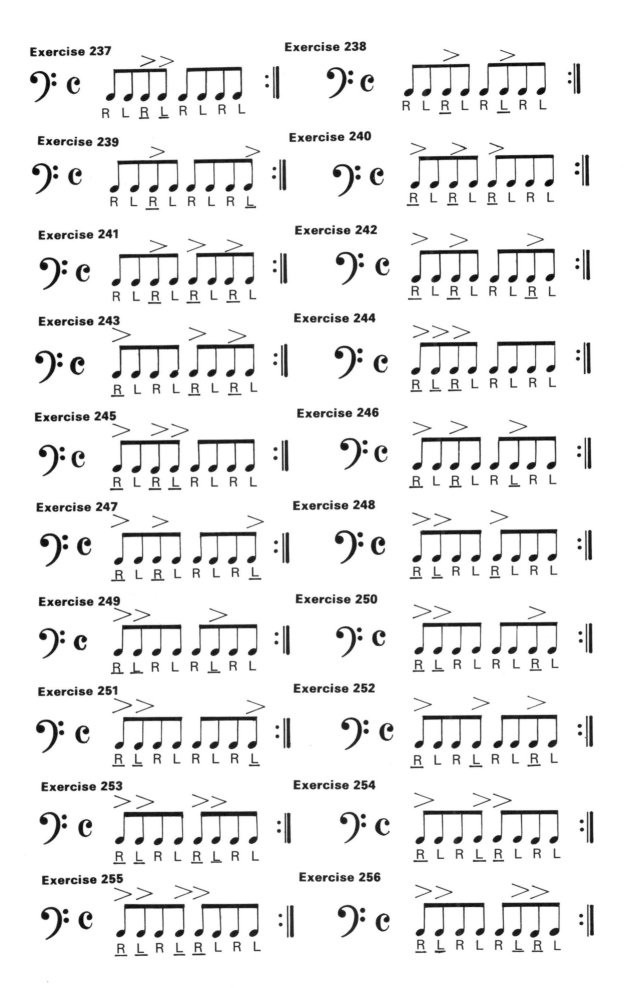

RIM SHOTS

Once you are happy with the accents studies you can try them again, this time making the accents into RIM SHOTS. As you can see from the illustration you should aim for the stick to strike both the drum head and the rim (or counterhoop) of the snare drum, thus producing a loud piercing tone . . . this rim shot technique may be easily applied to all the pop and rock rhythms learnt earlier.

Rim shots played with the right hand

Rim shots played with the left hand

AROUND THE DRUMS

Great benefit can be gained by applying the accent techniques learnt to create patterns around the drums. In the exercises that follow we are putting notes that would have previously been accents onto different drums.

Exercise 277

Exercise 278

Exercise 289

Exercise 290

Exercise 291

Exercise 292

Exercise 293

Exercise 294

Exercise 295

Exercise 296

Exercise 297

Exercise 298

Exercise 298(a)

Exercise 299

Exercise 299(a)

Exercise 300

R L R

Exercise 301

L R L

Exercise 302

R L R

Layout of the drum set.
Premier Resonator Drums and Avedis Zildjian cymbals supplied
courtesy of the Premier Drum Company of Leicester.

Fill-Ins for The Five Drum Set
(Taken from Contemporary Drum Fills)
by John Savage

Exercise A

Exercise B

Exercise C

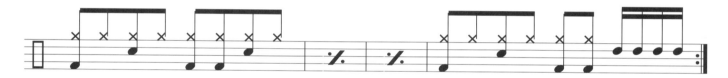

Exercise D

Exercise E

Exercise F

Exercise A

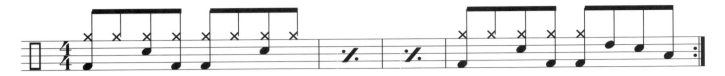

Exercise B

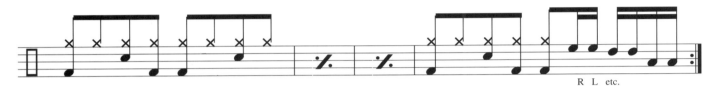

R L etc.

Exercise C

Exercise D

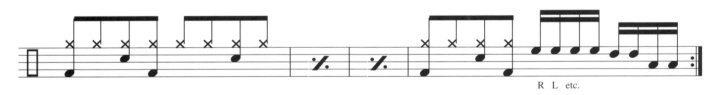

R L etc.

Exercise E

Exercise F

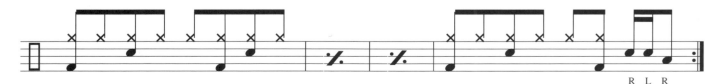

R L R

LESSON 14

STRENGTHENING THE LEFT HAND

In this chapter we shall play exercises and rhythms that demand greater skills from the left hand. Firstly, we play four snare drum exercises.

Exercise 303

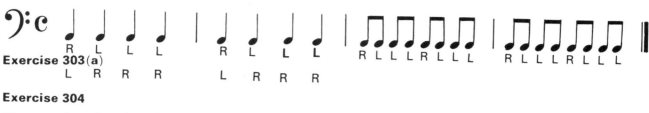

Exercise 303(a)

Exercise 304

Exercise 304(a)

Exercise 305

Exercise 306

B = Both Sticks together

Exercise 307

Exercise 308

53

Exercise 315

Exercise 316

Exercise 317

In the following exercises the snare drum playing four beats in each bar provides a solid driving rhythm.

Exercise 318

Exercise 319

Exercise 320

Exercise 321

Exercise 322

Exercise 323

If you experience difficulties with the bass drum part in exercises 322 and 323 then refer to Lesson 20 on Rock Drumming and study the techniques contained therein before returning to these two exercises.

BASS DRUM TECHNIQUE

At this point in our studies it is advisable for us to look at developing greater skill on the bass drum pedal. I have written no specific exercises for the bass drum but would recommend that you should play through most of the snare drum exercises encountered so far, playing each on the bass drum. Be careful to look at the way you use the bass drum pedal (see illustration) you should use the same approach for the bass drum as adopted for the snare drum; control the pedal with your foot so that the beater moves smoothly from its start position, strikes the head cleanly and returns immediately to the starting position. You should avoid 'kicking' the bass pedal footboard, as this makes the pedal difficult to control, by keeping your foot positioned on the bass pedal. If you strike the drum and leave the beater pressed against the drum head this will have the effect of dampening the sound of the drum; this is tolerable if you wish to dampen the ring of the drum straight away, but for normal playing the best tone will be obtained from the drum by bringing the beater straight back and allowing the drum to resonate freely.

Action of the bass drum pedal

LESSON 15

THE SNARE DRUM RUDIMENTS

Despite controversy concerning the value of the drum rudiments they are, without doubt, the next step that we must take in order to gain complete control over the drum set. However, these rudiments are seldom mastered easily, their full potential often takes weeks if not months of patient practice to realise. They are the corner stone on which higher degrees of proficiency are based

The Five Stroke Roll

There are two stickings commonly used for the five stroke Roll, double Stroke (which has its origin in military and traditional styles) and Single Stroke which is widely used in the modern music field today. BUT both stickings are important.

Exercise 324

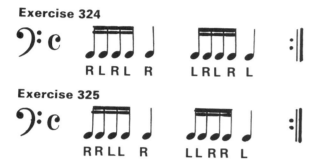

RLRL R   LRLR L

Exercise 325

RRLL R   LLRR L

Now we can repeat the rudiment with the basic foot pattern of bass drum, hi-hat, bass drum, hi-hat.

Exercise 326

Practice this exercise, either single or double stroke, until you can play it at a fairly bright tempo (♩=120) then leave out the hi-hat notes—this gives the rhythms a feel that you are now playing a slow four beats to the bar, with the bass drum playing on each beat. This means that your snare drum notes are now Demisemiquavers. (Eighth notes) See exercise 327.

Exercise 327

In Exercise 327 the five stroke Roll is best played with a slight emphasis on the First Note of each Roll. Whereas in Exercises 328 and 329 the emphasis comes on the Fifth note of each roll * ; thus the emphasis marks where the beat is.

*This emphasis could take the form of a Rim Shot.

Exercise 328

Exercise 329

We now play some snare drum exercises for the five stroke roll; in order that we save space we have printed  instead of this is a widely used abreviation that tells us to play demisemi-quavers to the value of a quaver (i.e. four 1/8th notes add up to a total of a half a beat.) Beneath each roll we place a Slur Line which tells us to play the roll as smoothly as possible. Try both Single and Double Stroke in each exercise.

Exercise 330

Exercise 331

Exercise 332

Exercise 333

Exercise 334

Exercise 335

Exercise 336

Exercise 337

Now we can move on to apply this rudiment to show its uses, both in fill-ins (short drum breaks) and around the drums.

Exercise 338

Note: the 5th note of the roll is played on the Ride Cymbal

(Stickings R L R L R or R R L L R).

Exercise 339

Exercise 340

R L R L R   L R L R L   R L R L R   L R L R L

To reach the Floor Tom-Tom cross the left hand *over* the right.

Exercise 340 (a)

R R L L R   L L R R L   R R L L R   L L R R L

Left hand crosses over the right when moving from the snare drum to the floor tom-tom.

In order to reach floor Tom-Tom in these exercises cross the left hand *under* the right.

Exercise 341

R L R L R   L R L R L ·   R L R L R   L R L R L

Exercise 341 (a)

R R L L R   L L R R L   R R L L R   L L R R L

Left hand crosses under the right when moving from the small tom-tom to the floor tom-tom.

Exercise 342

R L R L R   L R L R L   R L R L R   L R L R L

Exercise 342 (a)

R R L L R   L L R R L   R R L L R   L L R R L

Exercise 343

L R L R L   R L R L R

Exercise 343 (a)

L L R R L   R R L L R

Exercise 343 (b)

R R L L R   L L R R L

Exercise 344

L   R L R L R   L R L R   L   R L R L R

(Use the Crash Cymbal on the Left Hand Side of the kit for the first note)

Exercise 345

Exercise 346

Exercise 347

Exercise 348

60

Exercise 349

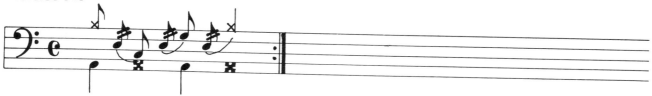

Variation on the Five Stroke Roll.

Exercise 350

The Six Stroke Roll

This rudiment should be an easy development from the Five Stroke Roll; but you should note that the hand chosen to lead will do so throughout, as opposed to the five stroke roll which changes from one hand to the other constantly.

Exercise 351   **Exercise 351(a)**

R L R L R L R L R L R L   L R L R L R L R L R L R

Exercise 351(b)   **Exercise 351(c)**

R R L L R L R R L L R L   L L R R L R L L R R L R

Exercise 352

Exercise 353

Exercise 354

R L R L R L

Exercise 354(a)
Repeat 354 sticking L R and note the left hand crosses *over* the right to reach the floor tom-tom.

Exercise 354 (b)
Sticking R R L L   R L

Exercise 354 (c)
Sticking L L R R L R (again use the crossover).

Exercise 355

R L R L R L

Exercise 355(a)
Sticking L R L R L R (To get to the floor tom-tom cross the left hand *under* the right).

Exercise 355(b)
Sticking R R L L R L

Exercise 355(c)
Sticking L L R R L R (again use the left hand crossing **under** the right to reach the floor tom-tom)

Exercise 356

R L R L

Exercise 356(a)
Sticking L R L R (cross left hand *under* the right).

Exercise 356(b)
Sticking R R L L (You will need to cross the right hand *over* the left in order to get back to the snare drum for the final roll).

Right hand crosses over the left when moving from the floor tom-tom to the snare drum.

Exercise 356(c)
Sticking L L R R (Cross left hand *under* the right to reach the floor tom-tom).

Exercise 357

R L R L R L (In bar 2 the left hand must cross *over* the right to reach the floor tom-tom).

Exercise 357(a)

Sticking R R L L (use the same crossover as before)

Exercise 358　　　　　　　　　　　　**Exercise 358(a)**

L R L R　L R　　　　　　　　　　L L R R　L R

NOTE: any of these Exercises may be played using Demisemiquavers simply by doubling the speed of the Stick Work.

Exercise 359

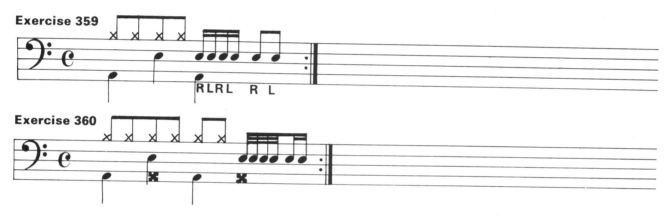

R L R L　R L

Exercise 360

The Seven Stroke Roll
This Roll is usually played in semiquaver form

Exercise 361

R　L R　L R L R　L　R L　R L R L

Exercise 361(a)　　　　　　　　　　**Exercise 361(b)**

R　L L　R R L L　R　L L　R R L L　　　L　R R　L L R R　L　R R　L L R R

Exercise 362

Exercise 363

Exercise 364

Exercise 365

R L R LRLR L RL RLRL R LR LRLR L RL RLRL

(Again the left crosses *over* the right to reach the floor tom-tom).

Exercise 365(a)
Sticking L R L R L R

Exercise 365(b)
Sticking R L L R R L L R

Exercise 365(c)
Sticking L R R L L R R L

Exercise 366

R L R LRLR L RL RLRL R LRLRLR L RL RLRL

There are two crossovers here; the left hand crosses *under* the right to reach the floor tom-tom and then to get back to the snare drum, when repeating, the right hand crosses *over* the left.

Exercise 366(a)
Sticking L R L R L R L R

Exercise 366(b)
Sticking R L L R R L L R (When repeating the right crosses *over* the left to reach the snare drum).

Exercise 366(c)
Sticking L R R L L R R L (The left hand crosses *under* the right in order to reach the floor tom-tom).

Exercise 367

.R LR LRLR L RL RLRL R LR LRLR L RL RLRL

Exercise 367(a)
Sticking L R L R L R L R (There are two crossovers here with the left crossing under the right to reach the floor tom-tom and the right crosses *over* the left to get back to the snare drum).

Exercise 367(b)
Sticking R L L R R L L R (The right hand crosses *over* the left to get back to the snare drum).

Exercise 367(c)
Sticking L R R L L R R L (The left hand crosses *under* the right to reach the bass tom-tom).

Exercise 368

R LR LRLR L RL RLRL

Exercise 368(a)
Sticking R L L R R L L R

Exercise 368(b)
Sticking L R R L L R R (The left hand crosses *over* the right to get to the floor tom-tom).

Exercise 369

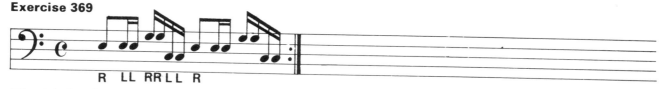

R LL RRLL R

(The left hand crosses *under* the right to reach the bass tom-tom).

Exercise 369(a)
Sticking L R R L L R R

Exercise 370

L RR LLRR

NOTE: that in this exercise the left hand crosses *over* the right in order to reach the floor tom-tom).

The Nine Stroke Roll

Exercise 371

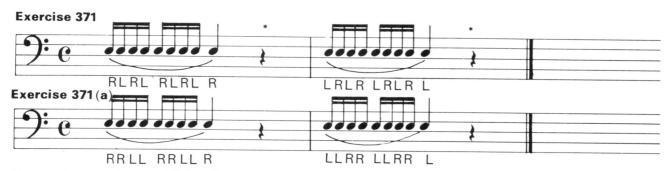

RLRL RLRL R   LRLR LRLR L

Exercise 371(a)

RRLL RRLL R   LLRR LLRR L

*Ensure that you leave a full beat's rest at the end of each bar

Exercise 372 *(Written)*   *Played*

Exercise 373

Exercise 374

Exercise 375

This Roll should be played starting with the right hand, whether single or double stroke.

Exercise 376

RLRL RLRL R   LRLR LRLR L

(Left hand crosses *over* the right to reach the floor tom-tom).

Exercise 376(a)

Sticking L R L R L R L R L   R L R L R L R L R

(This time the left crosses *under* the right in bar one to reach the floor tom-tom).

Exercise 37 6(b)

Sticking R R L L R R L L R   L L R R L L R R L (In bar two the left hand crosses *over*
      the right to reach the floor tom-tom).

Exercise 376(c)

Sticking L L R R L L R R L   R R L L R R L L R

Exercise 377

RRLL RRLL R

Exercise 378

LLRR LLRR L

The Ten Stroke Roll

Exercise 379

RLRL RLRL R L   LRLR LRLR L R

Exercise 379(a)

RRLL RRLL R L   LLRR LLRR L R

Exercise 380

RLRL RLRL R L   LRLR LRLR L R

Exercise 380(a)

RRLL RRLL R L   LLRR LLRR L R

Exercise 381

RRLL RRLL R L   LLRR LLRR L R

Exercise 382

RRLL RRLL R L   LLRRLLRR L R

In bar two the left hand crosses *over* the right to reach the floor tom-tom).

66

The Eleven Stroke Roll

Exercise 383

LL RR LL RRLL R

Exercise 383(a) as 383 but Sticking R R L L

Exercise 383(b)

LR LRLR LRLR L   RL RLRL RLRL R

Exercise 384

RL RLRL RLR L

Exercise 385

RL RLRL RLRL R   LR LRLR LRLR L

(In bar one the right hand crosses *over* the left to get back to the snare drum. In bar two the left hand crosses *under* the right in order to reach the floor tom-tom).

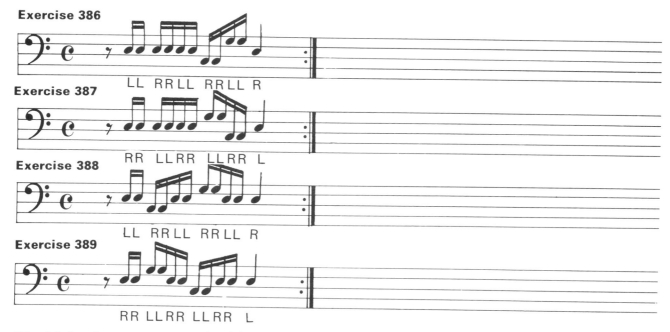

Exercise 386

LL RRLL RRLL R

Exercise 387

RR LLRR LLRR L

Exercise 388

LL RRLL RRLL R

Exercise 389

RR LLRR LLRR L

(The left hand must cross *over* the right to reach firstly the floor tom-tom and later the snare drum).

The Thirteen Stroke Roll

Exercise 390

LLRR LLRR LLRR L   RRLL RRLL RRLL R

Exercise 390(a)

RLRL RLRL RLRL R   LRLR LRLR LRLR L

Exercise 391

RRLL RRLL RRLL R   LLRR LLRR LLRR L

(In bar one the right hand must cross *over* the left to get back to the snare drum and in bar two the left hand must cross *under* the right to reach the floor tom-tom).

Exercise 392

RRLL RRLL RRLL R   LLRR LLRR LLRR L

(In bar two the left hand must cross *over* the right to reach the floor tom-tom).
(The same cross over comes in Exercise 392(a))

Exercise 392(a)

RLRL RLRL RLRL R   LRLR LRLR LRLR L

Exercise 393

RRLLRRLL RRLL R   LLRR LLRR LLRR L

Exercise 394

RRLL RRLL RRLL R   LLRR LLRR LLRR L

The Long Roll (Double Stroke)

Exercise 395

RRLL RRLL etc

(In bar one the right hand crosses *over* the left to return to the snare drum and in bar two the right again crosses *over* to reach the small tom-tom).

Exercise 395(a)
Sticking L L R R (In bar one the left hand crosses *under* the right to reach the floor tom-tom).

Exercise 396

RRLL RRLL

(The right must cross *over* the left in order to return to the snare drum when repeating).

Exercise 396(a)
Sticking L L R R (The left hand crosses *under* the right to reach the floor tom-tom).

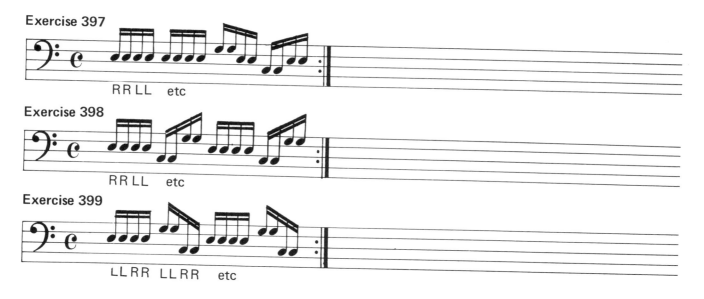

Exercise 397

RRLL etc

Exercise 398

RRLL etc

Exercise 399

LLRR LLRR etc

The Long Roll in Triplet Form

This rudiment is often difficult to master; the double stroke does not easily lend itself to triplets. You must practice slowly at first and make sure that you do not lose the triplet feel.

Exercise 400

R R L L R R L

Exercise 400(a)

L L R R L L R

Exercise 401

RRL LRR L etc

Exercise 401(a)

LLR RLL R etc

Exercise 402

RRL LRR etc

Exercise 403

RRL LRR LLR RLL

Exercise 404

RRL LRR LLR RLL

Exercise 404 (a)

LLR RLL RRL LRR

Exercise 405

RRL LRR LLR RLL

Exercise 405(a)

LLR RLL RRL LRR

(The left hand must cross *over* the right to reach the floor tom-tom).

In Exercises 403, 404 and 405, it would be a good idea to play a bar of swing rhythm prior to each exercise. In the case of Exercise 402 you would need to play two bars.

The Paradiddle

This rudiment is a particularly useful one

Note the use of accents

Exercise 406

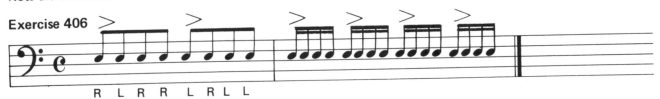

R L R R L R L L

We can play the Paradiddle in solos and fill-ins where the sound is lighter than single or double sticking.

Exercise 407

Exercise 408

RLRR LRLL

RLRR LRLL RLRR LRLL

Exercise 409

RLRR LRLL RLRR LRLL RLRR LRLL RLRR LRLL

Exercise 410

RLRR LRLL RLRR LRLL RLRR LRLL RLRR LRLL

Try combining Exercises 409 and 410 to create a four bar phrase.

Exercise 411

LRLL RLRR LRLL RLRR LRLL RLRR LRLL RLRR

Now you can try this accent variation :—

Exercise 412

Exercise 413

R L R R L R L L

R L R R L R L L R L R R L R L L

In order to further your musical phrasing you can try playing four bars of Rock Rhythm in front of exercise 409, 410 (repeated) or 411. Each time you are arriving at an eight bar phrase—if you combine all three exercises without stopping them you have 24 bars in all.

The Double Paradiddle

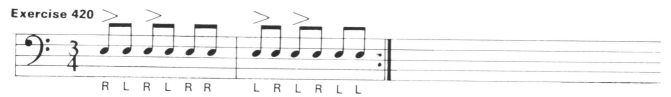

This rudiment occupies three beats so we can add another crochet (or equivalent notes) to make up our four beats to the bar.

The Flam

We now encounter a series of rudiments involving 'Grace Notes'. These Grace Notes are very light note(s) played immediately in front of the main note. The grace notes are crossed with a line to show that they have no time value and should be played as close as possible to the main note. As they are played quieter than this predominant note they give the effect of thickening and enhancing this main beat.

The Flam is a difficult rudiment to execute and requires much patient practice to perfect. Study the photograph carefully and you will see that we need to lift the right hand stick much higher than the left when executing exercise 430. Bring the two drumsticks onto the drumhead so that the Right stick strikes just after the left with a much louder note . . . each stick must return to its original position with the right hand high and the left remaining close to the drumhead. The left stick MUST STRIKE FIRST.

Exercise 430

The slur mark beneath each flam indicates the smoothness from one note to the next.

The Flam   IR

Exercise 430a will be much harder to master, but persevere and remember to lift the left hand stick high.

Exercise 430 (a)

The Flam   rL

73

In Exercise 430b we change hands in the middle of the bar and it is essential that you play each Flam from the correct starting position.

Exercise 430(b)

Exercise 430(c)

Exercise 431

Exercise 432

The Flam Accent : this rudiment will enable us to add flams to a triplet rhythm without altering the single sticking, but before attempting the complete rudiment we must first master some preliminary exercises.

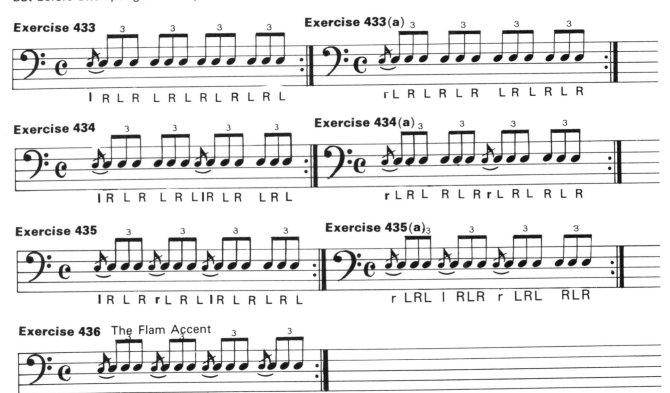

The Flam Tap: in this rudiment the flam is positioned before double strokes.

Exercise 437

I R R rL L I R R rL L

The Flam Paradiddle
Exercise 438

IR L R R rL R L L

THE CLOSED DRAG

This rudiment involves playing two grace notes immediately before the main beat, these two grace notes are played with one hand but should still be audible as two distinct notes.

Exercise 439

II R II R II R II R

Exercise 439(a)

rr L rr L rrL rrL

Exercise 439(b)

II R II R rr L rr L

Exercise 439(c)

II R rr L II R rr L

The Single Ratamacue
Exercise 440

II R L R L rr L R L R

The Double Ratamacue
Exercise 441

II R II R L R L rr L rr L R L R

The Open Drag
Although written the same as the closed drag the sticking of this rudiment lends it to modern music much more than its closed counterpart.

Exercise 442

Ir L rl R Ir L rl R

Exercise 443

The Closed Ruff

This rudiment involves three grace notes 'buzzed' with one hand prior to the main beat. This buzz is easiest played close to the rim of the drum where the tension is greatest. Again, be careful that the buzz is much quieter than the main note.

Exercise 444

rrr L   lll R   rrr L   lll R

Exercise 445

rrr L   rrr L   rrr L R L R   lll R   lll R   lll R L R L

The Buzz Roll

I could digress here and state that it is possible to play a form of drum roll known as the BUZZ ROLL using a similar technique to that used in the previous rudiment. In the absence of a fast double stroke you can simulate this effect by creating a long buzz first with one hand and then with the other. With practice this can easily be developed into a roll by closing up each long buzz; you do not have to play quickly, merely sustain the notes as long as possible. This roll is easier if played close to the rim of the snare drum to make maximum use of the tension of the drum and the effect of the snare.

The Buzz Roll

It is also possible to vary the closed ruff to make it more useable in pop rhythms. This variation is one handed only and consists of a buzz with the right hand, a light tap with the left hand and a very heavy note with the right hand (preferably a rim shot)

Exercise 446

rrr L R   rrr L R

To gain any effect this must be played in a very sharp and snappy manner

Exercise 447

rrr L

We conclude our rudiments section with the OPEN RUFF which is an adaptation of the triplet semiquaver exercises played in lesson twelve. Every aspect is identical except that the three lead-in notes must be phrased as closely as possible to the main beat.

Exercise 448

When we repeat this exercise the last note becomes the first beat of the Ruff.

Now try this Exercise

Exercise 454

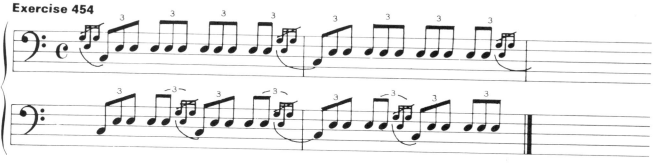

LESSON 16

Note Values

Before we can go on with further studies we must fill in any gaps left in our knowledge of musical theory etc. In previous exercises I have only explained enough theory to allow you to play each exercise as it appears but there are many other facets to written music and in this chapter we shall deal with different note values

We begin with notes that last for more than one beat. The Minim ♩ lasts for TWO BEATS, this note is easiest explained by imagining a trumpet player who has to blow a note and sustain it through two beats (two crochets) he is, thus playing a minim . The note that you play on the drum cannot last for two beats because the note dies very quickly once played, but if you keep the idea of this long note in your mind at the time of playing it is possible to phrase the notes fittingly.

Exercise 455

Exercise 456

Exercise 457

The Semibreve. This note lasts four Four Beats and would occupy a whole bar of four-four time.

Exercise 458

We could now write down a table of note values that shows the comparison between the notes that we have learnt so far. Each line adds up to a total of four beats, consisting of either One Semibreve or two minims or four crochets, etc.

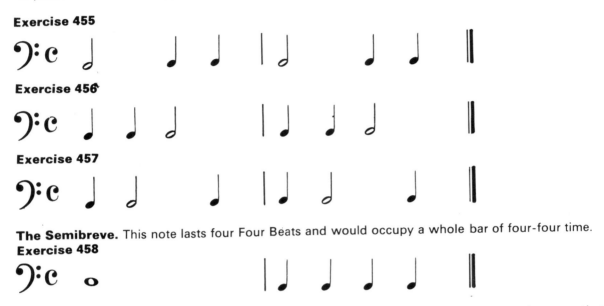

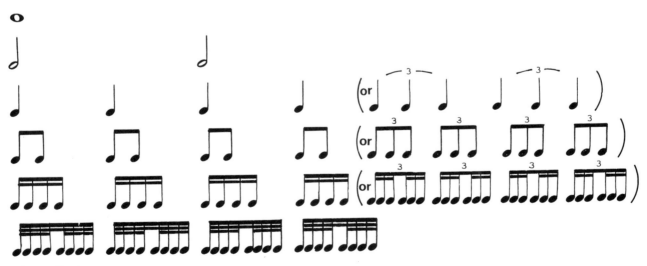

Rest Notes

Each of the notes that we have learnt has its equivalent Rest Note. The rest note represents an equivalent note of silence that is counted but not played on the drums.

The rest for a Semibreve is written

78

Often when there are several bars of rest this will be written as one rest bar with a number above it; the number represents the number of bars to be rested i.e.

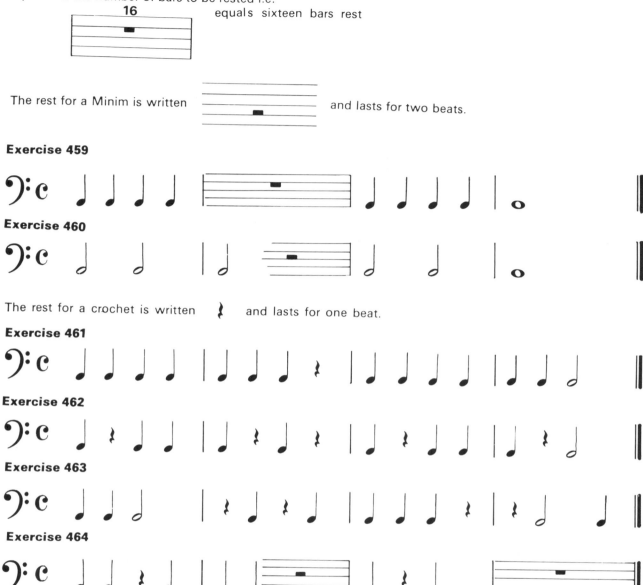

equals sixteen bars rest

The rest for a Minim is written and lasts for two beats.

Exercise 459

Exercise 460

The rest for a crochet is written and lasts for one beat.

Exercise 461

Exercise 462

Exercise 463

Exercise 464

If you want your playing to be musical then it is important that you listen to yourself and discern between long notes that Sustain like the Minim and Semibreve and notes that are followed by rest beats where you play ordinary notes followed by periods of silence.

The Quaver Rest is written and lasts for a half a beat. This may cause some problems at first, but work methodically through each exercise and you will soon master this rest note.

Exercise 465   **Exercise 466**

Exercise 467   **Exercise 468**

Exercise 469   **Exercise 470**

Exercise 471

Exercise 472

Exercise 473

Exercise 474

Exercise 475

Dotted Notes

A dot, placed immediately after a note, increases its value by a half again of its original value, i.e. a minim lasts for two beats, a dotted minim lasts for three beats.

Exercise 476

A crochet lasts for one beat and a dotted crochet lasts for one and a half beats.

Exercise 477

Exercise 478

Exercise 479

Dotted quavers have been dealt with earlier, but we can add the following exercises.

Exercise 480

Exercise 481

This particular phrase is more commonly written as 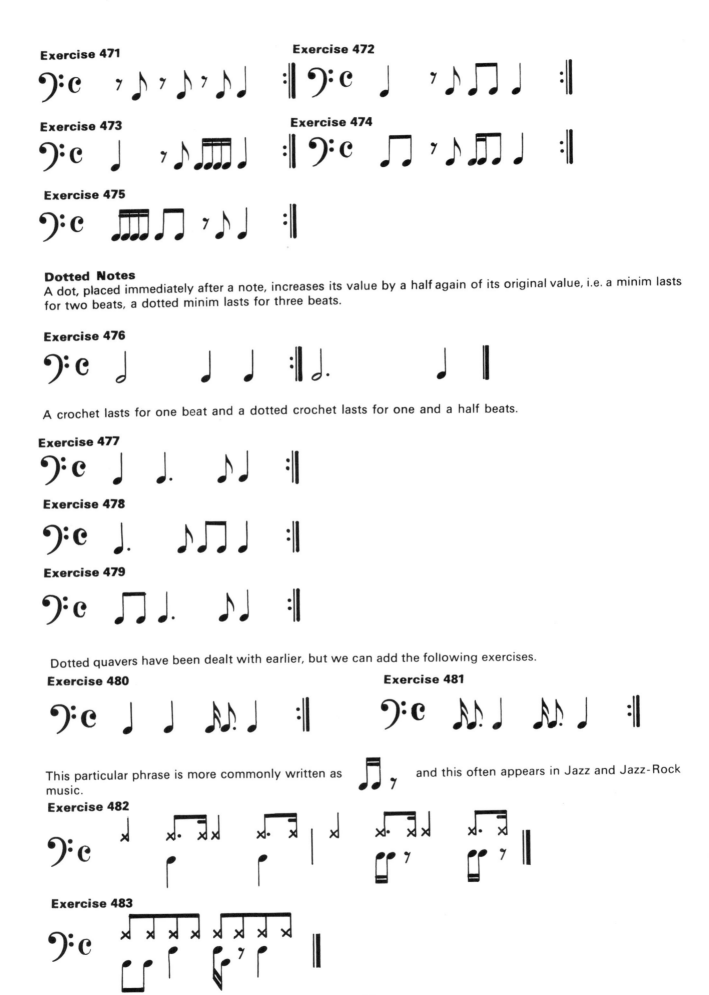 and this often appears in Jazz and Jazz-Rock music.

Exercise 482

Exercise 483

80

LESSON 17

TIME SIGNATURES

Until now we have concentrated our efforts on 4/4 or Common Time (four crochets to each bar) which is used in the vast majority of modern music. We must now understand other time signatures which, although not in such common useage, are important none the less. To understand the counting of these times we must know that a time signature is usually depicted by two numbers i.e. 4/4 of 2/4 etc., The top figure of the time signature tells us how many beats to each bar e.g. 4/4 means four beats to the bar; 3/4 means three beats to the bar, 2/4 time means two beats to the bar etc., the lower figure tells us what type of beats these are; this shows us what fraction of a semibreve each beat is . . . i.e. there are four Crochets to add up to one semibreve so a time signature with a four as the lower number must contain a number of crochets per bar (or the equivalent in other notes of course).(Thus 4/4 time means four beats to the bar, each of which is a crochet note of course).

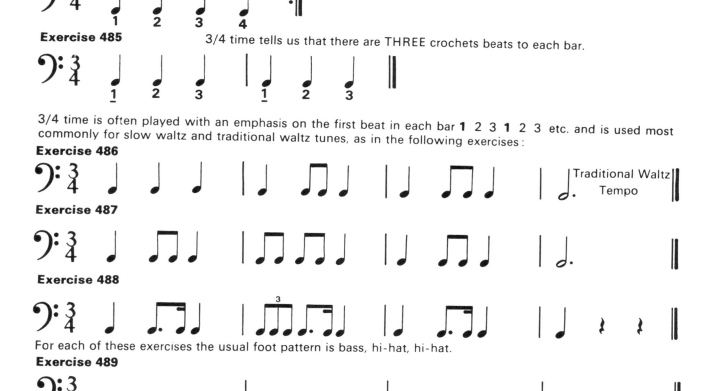

Exercise 484

Exercise 485   3/4 time tells us that there are THREE crochets beats to each bar.

3/4 time is often played with an emphasis on the first beat in each bar **1** 2 3 **1** 2 3 etc. and is used most commonly for slow waltz and traditional waltz tunes, as in the following exercises:

Exercise 486

Exercise 487

Exercise 488

For each of these exercises the usual foot pattern is bass, hi-hat, hi-hat.

Exercise 489

A detailed account of slow waltz rhythms is given in Lesson 18 which deals with Brush Rhythms. The Jazz Waltz is shown next and this can be played at medium and fast tempos.

Exercise 490   **Exercise 491**

Exercise 492

Exercise 493

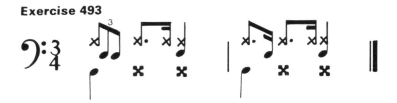

Rock Rhythms can also be played in 3/4 time.

Exercise 494

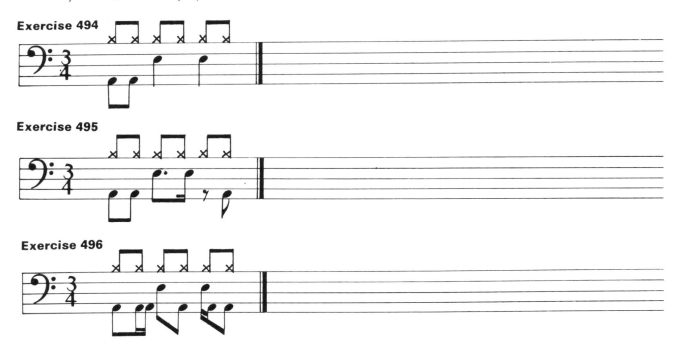

Exercise 495

Exercise 496

Two-Four Time means 2 crochet beats in each bar and is counted 1 2 1 2. This time signature is found most in military drumming where the marching pulse left, right, etc. is strong.

Exercise 497

Exercise 498

(5 Stroke Roll).

Five-Four Time means five crochet beats in each bar and is counted 1 2 3 4 5, 1 2 3 4 5. If you find it easier you can count 1 2 3 1 2 / 1 2 3 12 / etc. This time signature is only encountered rarely in the Jazz and Rock

Exercise 499

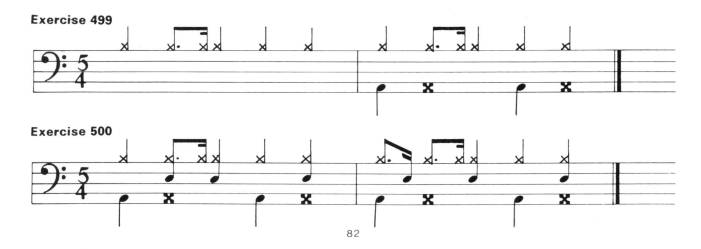

Exercise 500

82

Exercise 501

Exercise 502

Seven-Four Time

This time signature stands for seven beats to the bar each of which is a crochet. You may count this time as 1 2 3 4 5 6 7 / 1 2 3 4 5 6 7 etc. or split the bars up like 1 2 3 4 1 2 3 etc., to fit the phrasing of the piece. The exercises we shall encounter will be constructed in this manner (four beats plus three beats).

Exercise 503

Exercise 504

Exercise 505

Exercise 506

It should now be apparent that odd time signatures such as 9/4, 11/4, 13/4 can be worked-out fairly easily for yourself.

Three-Eight Time

This time signature contains three beats per bar each of these beats is a quaver (an eighth of a semibreve being a quaver).

Exercise 507

Counted   1   2   3   1   2   3   1   2   3   1

Exercise 508

Exercise 509

You may not encounter these odd time signatures very much, but their mastery will widen the scope of your playing.

Six-Eight Time
This means six beats to the bar, each of which is a quaver. This time signature has a strong link with military music and there is often an emphasis on the First and Fourth beats in the bar (marked in here with the bass drum)

Exercise 510

Exercise 511

Twelve-Eight Time
Means twelve beats in each bar, all of which are quavers. This time signature is used most commonly for slow ballad and blues songs and it is in this idiom that our exercises here are to be played.

Exercise 512

Exercise 513

Exercise 514

Exercise 515

You may note that time signatures like these can and often are broken down into groups of two s three s and fours for easier counting. For instance, 5/4 could be counted in a number of different ways according to the piece being played ; it could be 1 2 3 1 2 or 1 2 1 2 3. 7/4 time could be split up into 1 2 3 4 1 23 or 1 2 3 1 2 3 1 etc. and so on.

There are, of course, other time signatures in occasional use such as 9/8, 10/8 and so on, but I believe that the information given here should prove sufficient to allow you to cope with these as they arise.

CUT COMMON TIME

Cut Common Time (written 𝄵) is a much misunderstood time signature. It is usually encountered by the brass band, military, classical or orchestra pit drummer. The time signature is used to write very fast passages which would appear complicated in 4/4 time in an easier to understand fashion. The idea being that 4 beats to each bar are written but 2 only are played, so that the value of each note has to be mentally halved i.e.

instead of:—

The idea is that the 4/4 rhythm may be difficult to count as a very fast 1234 1234, whereas in Cut Common time it is easier to count a steady 1 2 1 2 and play each note twice as quickly as written.

LESSON 18

SWISH BRUSH RHYTHMS

The artistry involved in using wire brushes on the drum set is often overlooked by drum students, but this facet of playing is important from both a practical aspect and for the sake of technical proficiency. The student should feel free to adapt any of the examples given in this book to suit his own style, but this should only be done once the basic principles have been mastered.

The basic swish brush rhythm that is used for slow and medium swing numbers (i.e. Fox-Trot in the dance band) is the same in structure as that used for faster tempos (quickstep in the dance band). The right hand brush plays on the snare drum and uses the same rhythm as played previously on the ride cymbal.

Exercise 516

The bass drum and hi-hat parts can be added to this.

Exercise 516(a)

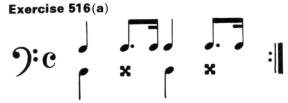

The left hand now sweeps around the drum head in rhythm . . .this is not written in our musical notation and there are two basic sweeps to use, determined by the speed of the tune. For slower tempos it is possible to sweep the left brush around the drum head one revolution per beat, bringing the tip of the brush toward the centre of the drum with each beat.

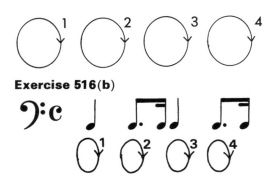

Exercise 516(b)

For faster tempos it sometimes isn't possible to sweep the left brush fast enough and we have to slow this down to half speed so that the brush reaches the centre of the drum on beat two and then again on beat 4. By bringing the left hand into the centre on the offbeats (at these points the two brushes are virtually one on top of the other) This helps to lift the rhythm more by emphasising these offbeats (2 and 4).

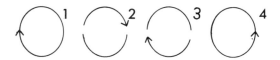

To help you master your brush work you should also work through any snare drum rudiments and exercises using brushes. Here now are some exercises in medium tempo for brushes, you may use either sweep with the left hand

Exercise 517

Exercise 518

Exercise 519

For very slow four-four and twelve-eight tempos you could find this rhythm helpful. It involves using the basic foot pattern and sweeping one revolution per beat on the left hand, while the right hand sweeps one revolution per beat in the opposite direction. If you bring both brushes together on the beat then the rhythm is held together better.

Exercise 520

A slow waltz rhythm is usually played with brushes, the sweep could be either one revolution per beat or per two beats. The basic foot pattern is bass hi-hat hi-hat and the right hand varies considerably but I have given you a basic example in Exercise 521.

Exercise 521

This rhythm can also be used for faster waltzes such as the traditional waltz, valeta, St. Bernard's etc. The basic fox-trot rhythm is also useable for Olde Tyme dances like the Palaise glide and Barn dance, etc.

Brush Rhythms

LESSON 19

LATIN AMERICAN RHYTHMS
Latin American rhythms are important, both to the dance band, and to the rock drummers. The dance band drummer needs to accumulate a comprehensive vocabulary of the most widely used latin rhythms, these he will use in a light, swinging fashion, whereas, the rock drummer will want to adapt them to use in a heavier rock style.

Bossa-Nova
The Bossa-Nova often proves difficult to many students so we shall build the rhythm up in stages. The right hand plays eight quavers to the bar on a tightly closed hi-hat cymbal whilst the left hand plays the snare drum part with the hand resting on the drum head and the stick striking across the rim to give a tight, click sound.

Exercise 522

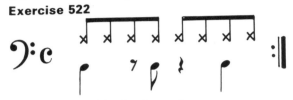

Now, add to this the bass drum.

Exercise 522(a)

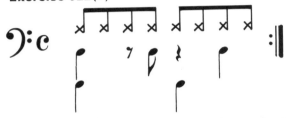

When you are completely happy with this rhythm you can try the full two-bar rhythm that is used most commonly for the basic bossa-nova.

Exercise 522(b)

Exercise 523

In Exercise 523 we vary the bass drum whilst maintaining the basic bossa pattern.

Don't be afraid to vary the pattern that you play to fit with any particular piece of music, but you must keep the 'Feel' of the bossa-nova, so listen hard to your playing and make sure that any improvisations you play are tasteful.

This rule can be applied to all latin rhythms, to adhere to the basic pattern all the time would be dull and uninteresting, but what you do play must fit in the context of what you are playing.

A softer sound for the boss-nova can be achieved if the right hand quaver rhythm is played with a brush on the snare drum. This rhythm can be varied further if the brush "swishes" quavers across the drum head instead of striking the drum, but you must maintain the quaver feel.

Cha-Cha
The Cha-Cha has a rhythmic feel of  throughout, but the rhythms that we shall play

will have a fuller sound whilst still maintaining the basic phrasing. Here are some suggested rhythms for the Cha-Cha, you would usually play the left hand stick across the Rim as we did in the Bossa Nova.

Exercise 524

The ride cymbal should be played on the 'Bell' (centre dome). To break the rhythm up the ride cymbal may be varied as in the next study.

Alternatively, you could use a cowbell instead of the ride cymbal.

Exercise 525

It is worth noting before we go on that the snare drum with the snares OFF gives you scope for playing tuneful fill-ins in latin-american numbers.

Samba

The Samba is a lively rhythm and we shall look at two different rhythms. The first is the easier to master, although it is a two bar rhythm we can study just the first bar and play this on its own. Master this first rhythm before attempting the complete two-bar rhythm.

Exercise 526

NOTE that the right hand plays all the tom-tom notes and the left remains on the snare drum.

Exercise 527

The Samba can also be played using the right hand stick on the ride cymbal bell. The left hand again rests on the drum head and the stick clicks across the rim.

Exercise 528

Exercise 529

The **Tango**: this rhythm is usually encountered by the dance drummer. I have written two studies here, the first is the basic rhythm and the second shows a fuller rhythm; you should adapt these basic rhythms to your own ideas. You may note that we use the five stroke roll extensively in this rhythm.

Exercise 530

Exercise 531

We conclude our Latin American section with two rhythms that are both played in the same easy, relaxed manner. In both rhythms you would play with the left hand resting on the snare drum, you are free to vary the pitch of the snare drum by pressing with this hand.

Exercise 532

The **Bolero**

Playing position for the Bossa Nova

Exercise 533
The **Rhumba**

Remember that you are free to vary each of these basic rhythms to suit individual tunes.

The Mambo

The Songo

LESSON 20

ADVANCED ROCK RHYTHMS

The history of percussion instruments dates back to the dawn of man's history, thousand's of years ago. From primative beginnings the snare drum, bass drum and cymbals could be found in use in the field of military drumming. But it wasn't until the twentieth century that the introduction of 'Swing' music and 'Jazz' demanded that the drummer play more than one drum simultaneously. The first drum sets were a weird and wonderful combination of snare drum, bass drum, cymbals, woodblocks, skulls etc., but these soon evolved into the sophisticated drum sets in use today. These advances have been demanded by the drummers that have progressed the art of drumming from its military base. The Jazz drummers have evolved much of the technique that we have learnt for Swing rhythms, but today, it is the Rock drummer who is expanding the art of the drummer even further. We shall now study some of the rhythmic techniques being used by top Rock drummers.

Exercise 534

Exercise 535

Exercise 536

Exercise 537

Exercise 538

Exercise 539

Exercise 540

Exercise 541

In the following exercises we use the Paradiddle sticking divided between the right hand cymbal rhythm and left hand snare drum.

Exercise 542

Exercise 543

If these rhythms are played using the hi-hat cymbals great effect can be achieved by opening and closing hi-hat cymbals.

A popular variation on our basic cymbal rhythm is now illustrated—this gives the rhythm an "up-beat lift" feel.

Exercise 544   **Exercise 545**

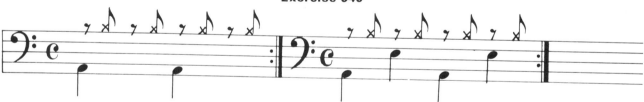

Exercise 546

Exercise 547

Exercise 548

Exercise 549

Exercise 550

Exercise 551

Exercise 552

Exercise 553

There are obviously countless variations on these rhythms which you should now try and evolve for yourself.

Hi-Hat Variations
There are three variations on our basic hi-hat pattern that we shall study here. We will only study basic rhythms, you should look to find more complicated rhythms as you progress.

Exercise 554

Hi-Hat ✗

Exercise 555

Exercise 556

Exercise 557

Exercise 558

Exercise 559

Exercise 560

Exercise 561

Exercise 562

Exercise 563

Exercise 564

Exercise 565

Exercise 566

Exercise 567

Exercise 568

Exercise 569

Exercise 570

Exercise 571

LARGER DRUM SETS

Today, the trend is moving more and more towards larger drum sets. I intend to build-up skill around larger drum sets in Volume II of The Art of the Drummer, but believe that before we can progress onto more drums it is essential that we gain a thorough mastery of the basic four drum set. This we have done in this volume.

SINGLE HEADED DRUMS

Another increasingly popular trend is the use of single headed drums. By removing the bottom head from any of your tom-toms or bass drum you will be able to increase the volume of your drum set. You will also change the sound of the drums ot a 'harder, flatter,' sound, and you must experiment with different tunings to obtain the sounds that you want from your drums.

RHYTHMS USING SINGLE STROKE SEMIQUAVERS ON THE HI-HAT CYMBALS

We conclude this chapter with some modern pop rhythms that use single stroke semiquavers played on the hi-hat cymbals. We play two warm-up exercises first and then a study that should give you plenty to work on. You may need to practice each bar separately and build-up to playing the completed study.

Exercise 572 RLRL etc

Exercise 573

Exercise 574

From Rock Drumming II

Exercise 54a

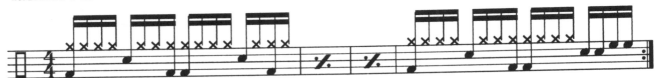

Sticking:- R L R L R L R L R L R L R L R L etc.   etc.   R L R L R L R L R L R L R L R L

LESSON 21

EXPRESSION MARKINGS

mp	Medium quiet	mf	Medium Loud
p	Quiet	f	Loud
pp	Quieter	ff	Louder
ppp	Very Quiet	fff	Very Loud

Cresendo (getting louder as the lines separate)

Decrescendo (getting quieter as the lines converge.)

Volume markings are often given on drum scores and they often look deceptively easy. Concentration is required to maintain a given volume once it has been established, for instance when an f or ff marking is given it is often the case that we go to the required volume but, after one or two bars start to let the volume die away back to your normal volume level; similarly, if given a quiet passage it is easy to let the volume creep up if you forget to maintain the required level of concentration and control.
The command of different volumes is very important in adding colour and depth to your playing, one of the best examples of this is to be found in drum solos where the player is so wrapped-up in the technical aspect of his playing that he forgets to vary the volume of the solo and it goes on and on in an undulating fashion that can make even the best technique seem boring. To be able to control the volume of your playing is as important an aspect of playing as technical ability itself. We begin our work in this chapter with eight basic volume control exercises.

Exercise 575

Exercise 576

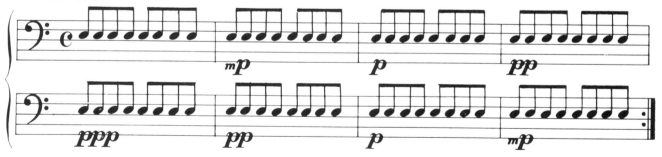

Exercise 577

We conclude this chapter by filling in one or two gaps left in our earlier work, which you may encounter from time to time.

D.C. means Dal Capo (go back to the beginning)
D.C. al ⊕ means go back to the beginning and when you reach the coda sign (⊕) go to the coda passage which will probably come at the end of the piece and be marked ⊕.
D.S. or D.𝄋 means go back to the sign rather than the beginning.

Tempo markings are usually given at the beginning of a piece.

Largo or Adagio	—very slow	Allegro	—Fast
Andante	—Slow	Vivace	—Lively, quick
Andantino	—medium slow	Presto	—Very Fast
Moderato	—moderate tempo	Meno Mosso	—Slower
Allegretto	—medium fast	Piu Mosso	—Faster

Changes in tempo:
     Ritardando or rit—gradually slower
     Rallentando or rall—gradually slower (often used at the end for finishes)
     A tempo—play at the previous speed.
     The Fermata or pause 𝄐 over a note means that it is sustained longer than its original value.

TIED NOTES

Thus far we have avoided the technique of 'tieing' one note to another although this is only occasionally used in basic drum music it needs to be understood by the drummer. It is common for arrangers to write out guide parts for the drummer which outline the basic structure of a tune and the arranger will often write phrasing guides for the drummer taken from the parts played by other instruments which may often include tied notes. Basically, if one note is tied to another then the first note is played and the sound of this should last through

the value of the second. i.e.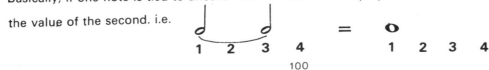

LESSON 22

TUNING AND CARE OF THE DRUM SET

The tensioning of the drums is not an easy process and one that relies upon skill that can only be gained through trial and error. The type of drum sound that you are seeking will vary much from individual to individual but the general rules apply to all.

The snare drum should be tensioned tighter than the other drums with the lower (snare) head tuned at least as tight if not tighter than the top (batter) head. The degree to which you tighten the drum will vary with the sort of sound that you want to get from the drum. If you like a flat sound then you will leave the heads fairly slack and also not overtighten the snares, like this the drum is less responsive. If you want a tight, crisp sound then you should tighten the drum more and also use the snares tight. The key to the quality of sound that you get from the snare drum (and indeed the whole kit) will depend upon the success that you achieve in tuning each drum head EVENLY. The best method is to tap the drum head close to one of the tensioning points and get the sound you want by adjusting the tension at this one point. Then go across to the other side of the drum and get the same sound at a point opposite to your start, keep tapping your original starting note to see that you do get the same sound. Repeat this procedure around the different tensioning points on the drum and you will arrive at an evenly tuned drum head. If both heads are evenly tuned then you will be playing the top head which is of an even pitch and the bottom head will resonate evenly in harmony with this note, the net result will be a clear, pleasant sound that projects away from you. A badly tuned drum means that several different sounds are created that don't resonate perfectly inside the drum and don't project a good sound, but instead a weak note that sounds tinny away from the drum.

The small tom-tom is tuned lower than the snare drum, if you can tune so that there is a pleasant drop in pitch between the two drums this will add to the effect (for the musically minded, a fourth is a good interval). For Jazz music this drum would probably be tuned fairly tightly, whereas for Rock it is often tuned slack. Remember that even tuning of the bottom head has much to do with projecting the sound of the drum so take your time with both heads.

The floor tom-tom is tuned again a nice interval lower than the small tom-tom (4th) and the same rules apply to tuning this drum.

The bass drum should be tuned with the same idea in mind, a slack batter head is used mostly today with the front head tighter for resonance. The test for each drum, especially the bass drum, is whether you can feel the sound projecting outwards from the front of the drum and not just bouncing straight back to you, the player.

The type of sound that you will get from your drums depends also on the style and manner of your playing, throughout the earlier pages of this book we spent considerable time with the playing action of the drum sticks. The whole technique that we have built-up has been aimed at achieving a clear, clean projecting sound and this sound will be altered by your own attitude towards the basic playing of the drums.

Maintainance of your drum set is quite a simple procedure. The outside of the drum shells should just be cleaned with an ordinary household polish and the chrome work is best cleaned with a non-abrasive metal or chrome polish. The tension bolt threads should be lightly oiled at regular intervals, say twice a year to keep them working efficiently and so should any necessary parts of the drum stands.

The replacement of drum heads is obviously to some degree a question of useage and finance, but for the best results drum heads should be changed regularly as they do lose both tone and response. The average semi-professional drummer would be best served by changing heads once or twice a year, whereas a professional would need to change more often and an amateur not as often. It is possible that the batter head on the snare drum will need changing more frequently than the other drum heads, but personally I have always favoured changing all the heads at one time ; new heads need a few hours playing to wear themselves in and lose their newness so I have always preferred to get this process over in one go.

Cymbals are often difficult to clean, the best method is to wash the dirt away thoroughly in warm soapy water and then clean with A NON-ABRASIVE cymbal polish, if this polish is also washed off with water and the cymbals dried they can then be repolished if necessary. Never use an abrasive cleaner as this can damage valuable cymbals. Time spent in cleaning cymbals is well worth-while as the sound is invariably improved with cleanliness Cases and careful packing of your drums and cymbals will repay you time and again as most damage is encountered in transit.

LESSON 23

ADDITIONAL TECHNIQUES

The following snare drum exercises may be added to your reportoire of drum technique and to your daily practice routine.

Exercise 583

Around the drums

Exercise 584

Exercise 585

Exercise 586

Exercise 587

R L R L R L R L R L R L R L R L R L R L R L R L R L R L

Exercise 587 (a)
L R L R L R L R L R L R L R L R L R L R L R L R L R L R

Exercise 587 (b)
R L R L R L R L R L R R L R L R L R L R L R L L

Exercise 587 (c)
R R L L R R L L R L R L R R L L R R L L R R L L

Exercise 587 (d)
L L R R L L R R L R L R L L R R L L R R L R L R

Exercise 587 (e)
R R L L R R L L R L R R L L R R L L R R L R L L

Exercise 588

L R R L R R L R R L R R

Exercise 589

L R R L R R L R R L R R L R R L R R L R R L R R

Exercise 590

R R L R R L R R L R R L

Exercise 591

R R L R R L R R L R R L

Exercise 592

L L R L L R L L R L L R

Exercise 593

Exercise 594

R L L R L L R L L R L L R

Exercise 594a

L R R L R R L R R L R R L

Exercise 595

R L L R L L R L L R L L R

Exercise 595a

L R R L R R L R R L R R L

Note: Be careful NOT to play these two exercises in triplet form, but try and keep to the quaver formation. You may also play the accents as Rim Shots or Tom-Tom notes.

LESSON 24
DRUM SOLO TECHNIQUE

Solos and drum breaks give the drummer a chance to use to the full technical ability he has achieved combined with his sense of muscianship to explore the full potential of the drum set. The studies that have gone before should stand you in good stead to create tasteful and interesting drum solos, that fit in the musical context in which they are set. The examples that are given to conclude this book are a) 'Fours', Four bars of rhythm alternating with four bars of solo. b) an eight bar drum break and c) a twelve bar solo. These are only meant as figures to fire your imagination to use the Four facets at your disposal, technique, musical phrasing, dynamic control and tonal range of the drum set, so as to create your own approach as the Art of The Drummer.

Exercise 596   **Fours in Swing Time**

* Remember that in the early stages of building your solo technique your feet should play the basic right left pattern to act as an anchor for your technique, which you can later develop into more intricate rhythms.

Exercise 597   **Eight Bar Solo (Building in Rock Rhythm).**

Exercise 598 Twelve Bar Solo.

RLRR LRLL RLRR LRLL

FUNKY DRUMMING

Is the latest addition to The Art of the Drummer Series. The book contains a thorough, yet easy to understand method for developing your technique in a funky drumming style. John Savage has recorded each exercise and rhythm in the book set into a funky musical background.

JOHN SAVAGE'S FUNKY DRUMMING

Book and cassette are available now from your music dealer. Or in case of difficulty write to John Savage's Music Books, 28 King George V Ave., King's Lynn, Norfolk PE30 2QF. Telephone 01553 770190.

New Titles in the Series include:

The Art of the Drummer Play-a-Long Cassettes
Drum Set Studies (for the Art of the Drummer)
Rock Drumming Book One
Rock Drumming Book Two
Rock Drumming Book Three
Rock Bass & Drums Play-a-Long Cassettes
Drum Solo Technique
Snare Drum Artistry